Cleopatra

The Queen Who Challenged Rome and
Conquered Eternity

(The Mystery Was Killing a Group One by One)

Carol Joseph

Published By **Regina Loviusher**

Carol Joseph

All Rights Reserved

Cleopatra: The Queen Who Challenged Rome and Conquered Eternity (The Mystery Was Killing a Group One by One)

ISBN 978-1-77485-603-1

No part of this guidebook shall be reproduced in any form without permission in writing from the publisher except in the case of brief quotations embodied in critical articles or reviews.

Legal & Disclaimer

The information contained in this ebook is not designed to replace or take the place of any form of medicine or professional medical advice. The information in this ebook has been provided for educational & entertainment purposes only.

The information contained in this book has been compiled from sources deemed reliable, and it is accurate to the best of the Author's knowledge; however, the Author cannot guarantee its accuracy and validity and cannot be held liable for any errors or omissions. Changes are periodically made to this book. You must consult your doctor or get professional medical advice before using any of the suggested remedies, techniques, or information in this book.

Upon using the information contained in this book, you agree to hold harmless the Author from and against any damages, costs, and expenses, including any legal fees potentially resulting from the application of any of the information provided by this guide. This disclaimer applies to any damages or injury caused by the use and application, whether directly or indirectly, of any advice or information presented, whether for breach of contract, tort, negligence, personal injury, criminal intent, or under any other cause of action.

You agree to accept all risks of using the information presented inside this book. You need to consult a professional medical practitioner in order to ensure you are both able and healthy enough to participate in this program.

Table of contents

Introduction 1

Chapter 1: Cleopatra's Early Life And The Origins Of Her Name 2

Chapter 2: What Race Was Cleopatra? .. 13

Chapter 3: Cleopatra's Rise To Power 19

Chapter 4: Cleopatra—Ruler And Queen 37

Chapter 5: Cleopatra's Personal Relationships 53

Chapter 6: The Children Of Cleopatra 70

Chapter 7: Cleopatra And The Roman War 86

Chapter 8: The Death Of Cleopatra 95

Chapter 9: The Timeline Of Major Events In Cleopatra's Life 104

Chapter 10: Cleopatra Through The Years—Popular Portrayals Of The Royal Queen 113

Chapter 11: The Legacy Of Cleopatra ... 122

Chapter 12: The Fate Of Egypt Following Cleopatra's Death 132

Chapter 13: The Earliest Known Days Of Cleopatra 137

Chapter 14: Her Father And How His Ruling Affected Her 143

Chapter 15: How Cleopatra Seized The Throne 149

Chapter 16: Cleopatra And Julius Caesar 164

Conclusion 183

Introduction

The story of Cleopatra has enchanted people for thousands of years. The love story alone is one that many have heard of, along with the bravery and courage that came from a woman trying to keep her country together on her own. This was a hard time for Egypt and it required a strong leader, something that many feared Cleopatra wouldn't be able to manage on her own. Many times her family tried to throw her off her rightful place on the throne in the hopes of getting the title and all the glory. Through this, Cleopatra prevailed, ruled her country, and had liaisons with some of the most powerful and well-known men in the Roman Empire. Interested? Look through this guidebook to find out more!

Chapter 1: Cleopatra's Early Life and the Origins of Her Name

Cleopatra, whose full name is Cleopatra VII Philopator, was considered the active pharaoh during the time of Ptolemaic Egypt. While her oldest son did reign for a short time as pharaoh, Egypt was on a downhill climb and became a province of the Roman Empire shortly after her death. As the last reigning pharaoh, there is a lot of mystery and intrigue that comes with this woman. While many of the stories may not be true, she still inspired a lot of awe from her people as well as those in other nations for being such a strong ruler.

Cleopatra comes from the Ptolemaic dynasty in Egypt. This is the group of Egyptians that began ruling Egypt after the death of Alexander the Great. During this rule, the pharaohs chose to speak in Greek rather than in Egyptian. Because the Ptolemaic dynasty chose to speak Greek, many of their court and official documents were also in this language, making it easier for scholars to understand what was going on.

Despite this, Cleopatra did learn her native Egyptian. As a ruler, Cleopatra chose to be represented as a reincarnation of Isis, an Egyptian goddess. She was not originally the ruler of Egypt in her own right, having shared the title with her father before his death and then with both of her brothers, one of whom she married. It wasn't until some time later that she held the title on her own.

It is unknown who Cleopatra's mother is. There are a lot of theories, and it is believed that she could have come from two different lines that were closely related. Since there was a lot of intermarrying between families and there were possibly two Cleopatras who were born and lived at the time, it is possible that her mother could be either one of these. Most people believe that her mother would have been Cleopatra V Tryphaena, from Egypt. Even if this is not her mother, her mother would be from another part of the Ptolemaic family.

There are some who speculate that Cleopatra was the daughter of a slave. It was not uncommon for royalty at that time to take on a mistress or a slave and have children with them. Some historians believed that Cleopatra was such a child, and this is why she was able to easily learn the Egyptian language. This theory has been questioned, though; if Cleopatra had been born to an Egyptian slave, questions about her legitimacy would have arisen, especially when the Romans were angry with her. None of these claims ever showed up, leaving many to believe that she was the daughter of one of the Cleopatras in the Ptolemaic family.

It is better known who Cleopatra's father was: Ptolemy XII Auletes. This man was one of the direct descendants of Ptolemy I Soter, one of the best generals of Alexander the Great. Auletes and Cleopatra's mother are thought to be either cousins or siblings. This was not uncommon in many royal families, especially for those in Egypt. This helped to keep the bloodline pure and insured that there would not be any questions as to who belonged on the throne. This would eventually allow for

Cleopatra and her brother to continue the line by marrying and taking over the throne together.

As mentioned, Cleopatra started her rule by helping out her father. Her father trusted her judgment. He wanted to make sure that Cleopatra understood how things worked in the country and that she would be able to take on the role of ruler.

Cleopatra spent a lot of time with her father, traveling to other parts of the world as a young girl. Before even becoming a co-ruler, her father took her to Rome to help set up relations that would prove beneficial to keeping Egypt free from captivity. This helped Cleopatra in later years. She learned Roman customs, language, and traditions, making it much easier to hold on to the relationships that she is well-known for later in life.

Once Cleopatra's father died in later years, she also helped to rule along with her brothers Ptolemy XIII and Ptolemy XIV. She married both of them. Once her brothers died, she took over the throne and became

Egypt's sole ruler. She held onto the throne for quite some time and ensured that she had an heir to take over.

One move that helped to solidify her as the true ruler was her liaison with Julius Caesar. Through this liaison, she bore a son whom she called Caesar. While Julius never did claim her son as his own, he was probably's the boy's father, as he and Cleopatra were involved at the time. Cleopatra later added her son as a co-ruler once he was old enough to start learning more about the throne.

This was not the only liaison that Cleopatra had during her years on the throne. Once Julius Caesar was assassinated, she began to set her sights on Mark Antony. Antony was challenging the legal heir to the throne, Caesar's son Gaius Julius Caesar Octavianus (he later became known as simply Augustus). There are several theories as to why Cleopatra would oppose her ex-lover's heir. The first theory is that she believed her son, Caesar, should be the one on the throne. She had always claimed that this son belonged to the Roman line of succession, and it would have further solidified her claim to her own throne to be associated with the Roman Empire.

The other theory is that, if her son was not able to take over the throne, then she wanted to be close to someone else who could take care of her. Things were not going well for countries that were going against the Roman Empire. Cleopatra had been working to keep her country independent, but knew that if she was on the wrong side of things, she could end up having her country taken over. Augustus would not be the answer to this dilemma, as he already knew Cleopatra as his father's mistress. Perhaps Cleopatra saw Mark Antony as the answer that she needed.

Regardless of which theory is the right one, Cleopatra aligned herself with Antony and had three children with him. The first were a set of twins, Alexander Helios, and Cleopatra Selene II. Later on, she had an additional son with Antony named Ptolemy Philadelphus. It is interesting to note that Cleopatra never bore children from either of her marriages with her brothers, only from her relationships with Julius Caesar and Mark Antony.

Cleopatra and Mark Antony soon started to make the leader of the Roman Empire, Octavian, angry. He was the sole ruler of the country but had split up the provinces and given some to Antony as a sign of trust and loyalty. But with Cleopatra by his side, Antony ended up taking things too far. He decided that he had just as much right to the throne as Octavian and tried to help Cleopatra's son, the one who was born from Caesar, get to the throne.

Together, Antony and Cleopatra flaunted their power and their beliefs in front of Octavian, throwing lavish parties where they declared Cleopatra's children as the true rulers of the area and kings of kings. This angered Octavian, who was worried that he would lose his place as the rightful ruler. Soon Cleopatra and Antony were no longer safe and had to flee.

After a number of years, things started to turn bleak for Mark Antony. He lost his battle with Augustus at the Battle of Actium. After this defeat, Antony decided to commit suicide rather than let Augustus get ahold of him and torture him. Soon after the suicide of Antony, Cleopatra decided to follow suit. Cleopatra killed herself in 30 B.C. using an asp bite.

Once Cleopatra was dead, her son Caesarion took over the throne. He had been serving as the co-ruler with his mother for a number of years at this time and had a good idea of how to make things work. He had quite a few supporters, all of whom were happy to name him pharaoh. But things were looking bleak by this time. Augustus was not happy that Cleopatra had been working against him in his fight to take over Rome. He decided to take his anger out on Egypt. He did this by killing Caesarion and then taking over Egypt, which became a Roman province, Aegyptus.

Cleopatra was an oddity in her times. At the age of 14, she had already traveled with him to help out with peace meetings in Rome, and despite his fear that someone else in the family would try to overthrow him, Ptolemy XII still chose to name his daughter as co-ruler. In that time, it was unusual for a father to choose a daughter, especially one who was so young, to help rule the country.

Even later in life, after being married to her brother, Cleopatra refused to step down from her role. She was used to ruling the country and did not feel that she deserved to be second best. When she was expected to be subservient to her brother and to bring back the Ptolemy name on official records, she refused and ended up in exile until Caesar helped her out.

The story of Cleopatra has been captivating people for years. The idea of such a strong figure, who outlived many other famous rulers and was able to hold her own, has intrigued and fascinated all sorts of people. In fact, people from the Western world are even more fascinated by this last ruler of Egypt than the Egyptians themselves. It is easy to find the legacy of Cleopatra in literature and art.

The Origins of A Name

The name "Cleopatra" is Greek, meaning "she who comes from glorious father". This may also have been a name that was passed down by other women in her family.

While the exact lineage of her mother is unknown, it is assumed that her mother is one of the Cleopatras in the Ptolemaic family. The families in Egypt often intermarried, which helped to keep the line pure but often made it difficult for historians to keep track of everyone.

While it is unsure which of the two Ptolemaic Cleopatras her mother was, it is pretty certain that this name had been carried down for many generations. And named her daughter after herself as well, much like the men of the time who passed down their names to their heirs.

While she was the first one to hold this name in her generation, she is known to be the third daughter of Ptolemy XII. Once her father died, Cleopatra continued to rule along with her brother Ptolemy XIII. Lines to the throne could only pass on the mother's side, so marrying her brother allowed him to become king.

Chapter 2: What Race Was Cleopatra?

Throughout history, people have wondered about the race of Cleopatra. This has sparked a lot of debates over the years about what Cleopatra would look like, whether she would get along with her people, and what her ruling style would be like. Portrayals of Cleopatra vary depending on who is the artist and the way she has been painted has varied a lot throughout history. The biggest debate about Cleopatra's race is between the Afrocentric historians and Egyptologists.

First, let's look at what the Egyptologists have to say. They believe that Cleopatra is one of the descendants of the Ptolemaic dynasty. This is a family that comes from Macedonia and is descended from Ptolemy I Soter, one of the generals of Alexander the Great. When Alexander was done creating his empire, he had left the area of Egypt to Ptolemy. The whole family of Ptolemy came from Macedonian royalty and they brought a lot of their traditions and culture to Egypt with them.

The fact that the Ptolemaic family liked to marry between themselves leads these historians to believe there is not much chance that outside regions and cultures would be added into the family tree. Plus, the Macedonian family that took over never had much use for even learning the Egyptian language at the time and stuck with Greek. Cleopatra was the first in her family to even learn some of the Egyptian language. The background and family tree of Cleopatra seems to point to the fact that she would have been white.

Added to this is the fact that all of the depictions of Cleopatra from that time, including the coins that pictured her face, her ancient busts, and many of the paintings that she had commissioned, depicted a woman with fair skin. Some descriptions of Cleopatra show her as a girl with reddish brown hair, a hawk nose, who was a bit overweight and pretty short for her age.

On the other side of things, Afro-centric historians believe that she may have been partly black. This is brought up mainly because of the fact that the identity of Cleopatra's mother is not known for certain. They claim that Egypt, both now and in ancient times, was mostly full of black people, being that it was an African country. While they do agree that the Ptolemy family was white, they believe that at some time there were sexual liaisons between the people of Egypt and the monarchs.

This is not such a hard thing to imagine. Monarchs in all countries had mistresses and others they slept with on the side. While most of the time the children of these relationships were not offered the throne or given positions of power, it did help the king to have more children, in case he was not able to produce an heir for the throne. It is possible that through these lines, one or more of the pharaohs had relations with a native of Egypt and produced an heir.

If this is true, it is possible that Cleopatra may have been at least partly black. It is known that her father is white so her being completely black is not a reasonable assumption, but since the name of Cleopatra's mother is kept out of the Ptolemaic family tree, it is not impossible that her mother may have been black.

One possible candidate for Cleopatra's mother is Cleopatra V Tryphaena, the sister of Aulete. This theory is given even more credence considering that the legitimacy of Cleopatra being on the throne was never questioned, even though her brother Ptolemy and the Romans published a lot of propaganda against her.

Why is this important? To start, if Cleopatra had been born to a black slave or another person who was not a part of the Ptolemaic family, this information would be released early on. It would mean that Cleopatra technically had no claim to the throne, even if her father wanted her to take over once he was gone. While Cleopatra was beloved by her own people, there were a lot of people of power in her life that didn't like her and worked hard to dispose of her. If she held no legitimate claim to the throne, those against her would have announced this right away.

It is also unlikely that her father would have ever named Cleopatra as his heir if she was not legitimate. She did have another sister, Arsinoe IV, who could have been declared the legitimate heir rather than Cleopatra. It only makes sense that Cleopatra at least came from a line that gave her a right to the throne. Finally, the Romans, some of her biggest enemies after Caesar died, never did describe her as a black person. The Romans were particularly hard on blacks during this time and would have used anything in their arsenal against Cleopatra in order to attack her. If she were black, they would let others know it as a way to make it easier to take over. In none of the Roman histories is Cleopatra ever described as a black woman.

The debate about the racial identity and skin color of Cleopatra might not seem all that important, but it is a great example of cultural and identity politics. The idea of cultural politics is that there is a huge cultural bias in historical accounts based on race. For example, there is a lot of history that credits African achievements to Europe.

Would Cleopatra have been as successful if the family wasn't into interbreeding and she had been born black? With the way that history pans out, it is unlikely that she ever would have gained the favor of the Romans, especially Caesar, and her brother would probably have got ahold of the throne instead of her.

Chapter 3: Cleopatra's Rise to Power

Cleopatra was the rightful queen to the throne thanks in large part to marrying her brother, being the eldest daughter of the previous king, and the experience she had as a ruler both while her father was alive and as the wife of her brother. She had the experience to know how to run Egypt in difficult times. Remember that the Roman Empire was beginning to grow and take over as much of the world as it could; this would include the prosperous area of Egypt.

This meant that Cleopatra had a lot of work to do before she could take over the country. The way that Cleopatra made it to the throne was not pretty. He father had one of the worst dynasties in their history, and there was a lot of fighting and corruption amongst the government and its officials. Corruption and centralization of power were two of the main issues during Ptolemy XII's reign. In fact, these are the reasons that there were uprisings in Cyrenaica and Cyprus that resulted in the pharaoh losing both of these provinces.

Things did not get worse once the Roman Empire began to spread. The leaders of this empire were determined to have one of the best empires in the whole world, even bigger than that of Greece, their predecessors. They had already taken over a lot of other countries that had once belonged to Greece, and they were looking around to take over more countries. Egypt would have been the perfect choice for them. It was full of great land, easy access to the Nile, and other great rivers and lakes that could help with trade, and the culture was something to brag about.

The different provinces of Egypt were not getting along that well at the time. Some groups were not happy that they were being led by a family that was not from their country originally and who didn't even take the time to learn their language and customs. Others were very interested in joining with the Roman Empire and wanted to be free of the Ptolemaic family once and for all. The most damaging thing to the country was the economic turmoil. People were tired of the famine and drought, and some hoped that a new ruler might be able to help them put food on the table.

Ptolemy XII understood that it would be pretty easy for the Roman Empire to come after them. Egypt, while a strong and proud country, would never be able to withstand the power of the Roman Empire. Ptolemy XII decided to pursue a different tactic: being friends with the Romans. He figured that showing friendship to the country and offering them trade and use of their resources would help to keep the country in the hands of the Egyptians. If the Romans were getting everything they wanted already, they might move their military resources somewhere else.

With this thought in mind, Ptolemy and Cleopatra went to Rome to make some connections with its rulers. Things in Egypt did not go very well while they were away. Cleopatra VI Tryphaena took over the throne and acted as the pharaoh for a time. Unfortunately, this Cleopatra did not survive long afterward. While no one is sure why she passed on, her death has been considered suspicious, and many believe that Berenice IV poisoned her to get the crown for herself.

Berenice had always wanted to hold on to the throne, but she was too far removed once Cleopatra was born. She finally saw her chance to become ruler when Cleopatra and Ptolemy XXII left the country. She knew that if she was able to get the interim ruler out of the way she could take over the crown for a time. There are theories that Berenice poisoned the interim pharaoh and had plans to take the crown, garner supporters, and kick Cleopatra and Ptolemy out of the kingdom if they ever did return.

Of course, most of this is just theory. Either way, Berenice held on to the crown for some time until Cleopatra and Ptolemy finally came back from Rome. They had been pretty successful during their time in Rome and got the support they had been looking for. They had gotten the support of Aulus Gabinius, a

Roman general, who helped them to capture Alexandria.

This backstabbing was common at the time. There were too many people that were close to the crown, and the second that there was some weakness among one of the members, someone was happy to jump in and try to take over. Not only would this have happened within the royal family; others in the general populace had tried, albeit unsuccessfully, to take over the crown.

When the two got back, Ptolemy was not happy with his daughter Berenice. He had heard many of the rumors of what had happened during his time away, and he did not like the way that his daughter was attempting to rule the country. Berenice was quickly imprisoned and then executed by order of her father. According to legend, her head was then sent around the royal court. Whether this is true or not, it is thought this action was done to keep the other royals in line and to prevent them from trying to take the throne for themselves.

At this time, Cleopatra then became the joint regent as well as deputy to her father. While she had shown herself worthy while in Rome, her father was afraid that she might take on too much power and try to bring harm to him. Because of this, Cleopatra had a lot of limits on her power and was the head of state only in name.

It took a long time before Cleopatra was able to get more power. During her father's lifetime, she was basically in the background. It is believed that Ptolemy spent some time training his daughter and getting her ready to take up the throne. If the royalty and the country were not in such turmoil, it is likely that Cleopatra would have had more power at a younger age. As things were, Cleopatra was not able to attempt total power until after the death of her father and her co-reign with her younger brother.

Just four years later, in 51 B.C., Ptolemy XII died. He had left a will behind to help determine who would take over the throne once he was gone. While succession was usually determined by birth order, things were getting bleaker in Egypt, and many thought the will was a formality that helped to keep uprisings and other issues from happening. At the age of 18, Cleopatra, and her brother, Ptolemy XII, who was just 10 at the time, became joint monarchs.

The beginning of their reign together was hard on them. First off, there were a lot of horrible floods in the Nile area, famine, and economic failures. The people were crying out for help, and some had even turned to Rome, thinking that this was the way out of the trouble they were facing. Political conflicts soon began to arise, and Cleopatra and her brother had to work hard to keep hold of their country. With Cleopatra's experience, and the fact that her brother was so young, Cleopatra soon set herself up as the sole ruler and did not share the power well with her younger brother, which made him, and his advisors, very upset that a woman was taking over.

This ended up causing some tension before the siblings and spouses. In 51 B.C. Ptolemy and Cleopatra's relationship completely broke down. Cleopatra decided that she no longer needed to have the traditional Ptolemy name associated with her and she began to take this off all of her official documents. In addition, she started to change the coins that were given out in Egypt, making sure that her face was the only one that showed up on the coin. This was not something that was allowed in the traditional Ptolemaic Egypt; in this tradition, the female rulers would be considered as subordinate to their male co-rulers. By contrast, Cleopatra was stating that she was on the one in control and that she would not be lower than anyone else, regardless of her gender.

Then, in 50 B.C., Cleopatra started having conflicts with a group known as the Gabiniani. These were some powerful troops from the Roman Empire, who had had been left in Egypt after Aulus Gabinius helped Ptolemy XII win back his empire a few years before. The

Gabiniani killed off the sons of Marcus Calpurnus Bibulus, one of the Roman governors present in Syria, when they asked for help against the Parthians.

Cleopatra remembered how much the Romans had been of help to her and her father a few years before, and she understood that she needed to be a partner with them in order to rule her country. She dealt harshly with these murders and handed them over to Bibulus in chains. This did not make the Gabiniani happy, and they soon became enemies to Cleopatra. This was considered one of the main reasons why Cleopatra fell from power.

Shortly after this, Ptolemy XIII forced Cleopatra to leave her throne. He was not happy that his sister and wife, who was supposed to be subservient to him, had decided to take on so much control. He had allowed this to go on for a few years, as he was a younger king and felt that his sister, with more years and experience, would be better suited to rule.

But as the king got older, he became more aware of the amount of power that his sister had, and he wanted to regain the power he believed belonged to him. When Cleopatra tried to establish herself as the sole heir to the throne, Ptolemy decided it was time to take a stand. He drove his sister out of the palace in Alexandria.

There is some speculation as to whether Ptolemy was the one to put out the orders for Cleopatra to be banned, or if his advisors were the root of the problem. As Ptolemy came to power as a co-ruler at age 10, he had several advisors who were there to help him make decisions and to learn how to rule. It is widely believed that several of his advisors had ideas of becoming rulers themselves and enjoyed the power they held over the young king.

These advisors soon became upset when they weren't able to control Cleopatra in the same way. They liked their power and felt that if they could control the king, it shouldn't be too hard to control his wife, a female that really shouldn't have any power. When Cleopatra refused to back off and still wanted to rule the country, the advisors became mad and bent the ear of the young king in order to convince him that his sister was a traitor and misbehaving.

Being only 20 or so at the time, Cleopatra left and went to Syria. After some time, she came back with a simple army and who set up camp right by the capital.

This was when Julius Caesar began to take notice of Cleopatra. At the time, he was going after another military rival who was on their way to Egypt as well. He was slowly drawn into this feud within the Egyptian royal family. He knew that Rome was stronger than Egypt but that they were the subservient ally that Rome needed when it came to keeping the Nile Valley stable and providing Rome with a lot of the food that they needed. He decided that it was his place to get in the middle of this feud.

In an attempt to help, Caesar took up residence in the Alexandrian palace for a time and tried to get both of the warring siblings to come in for a peace conference. Caesar planned to be the arbitrator of this meeting. He fancied himself as the most powerful man in the world at the time, and he was probably right, and so he felt it would be logical process for him to take over negotiations. Ptolemy was not having any of this, though, and his troops refused to allow Cleopatra to come anywhere near the castle in Alexandria, effectively making it impossible for a peace conference to happen.

Cleopatra, well versed in the relationships between Egypt and Rome, and understanding that Caesar could be just the ticket that she needed in order to get back on the throne, decided she needed to sneak into the castle in order to meet Caesar. Cleopatra got one of her servants to wrap her into a carpet or a sack, depending on the story you go with. This was then presented as a present to Caesar.

When Cleopatra was able to get into the room with Caesar, he was impressed. He decided to help out Cleopatra, and she slowly was able to regain her place on the Egyptian throne. Ptolemy did not take this lightly, and he decided to rebel against Caesar. This did not go well for Cleopatra's brother; during this civil war, the Nile began to flood again, and it is believed that Ptolemy perished in the river. This left Cleopatra alone to rule the throne.

Luckily, Cleopatra had some idea of what was going on in the world. Things were not going much better for her than they had been for her father, in terms of strife, uprisings, and unrest. Despite having the support of the Roman Empire for the time being, Cleopatra had to keep up with the front and make sure they did nothing to offend the Romans. One affront and there could be all-out war to deal with.

It was lucky that Cleopatra spent so much time with her father, going to Rome and learning how to run the country. She spent quite a bit of her time as queen, especially during the time that she was the sole queen, in Rome, working to keep relations open with the rulers there. She did have the unique advantage of being a woman and having something different to offer the men of the court, including Julius Caesar and Mark Antony. Many speculate that she may have entered these relationships, and had children with both leaders, in the hopes that she would be able to keep their ties strong.

There is speculation about how Cleopatra was able to convince Caesar to pay attention to her. Any other woman who tried to sneak into a meeting like that would have been exiled and thrown out of the room. But when Cleopatra arrived, Caesar was amused and took her side. Some say it is because of Cleopatra's beauty, while others point to her charm, wit, and diplomacy. Others still think that Caesar was impressed by her ancient lineage and wanted to know more about her on his own. Regardless of the reason, the two hit it off and became lovers for the rest of Caesar's reign in Rome.

While on the throne, Cleopatra bore a son to Caesar, but since he already had a wife, she was not able to marry him. Cleopatra continued to follow the customs in her country and married her other brother, Ptolemy XIV. This went on for a few more years, with Cleopatra mostly taking on the reigns as queen and her brother staying in the background. But when Caesar was killed in 44 B.C., Cleopatra soon realized that her best ally and friend was gone. She worried that she would not have the same hold on another Roman emperor and that someone would try to take away her and her son's claim to the throne.

Rather than letting this happen, Cleopatra ordered that her brother and second husband be killed. This helped to get rid of any challenges that she may have had to face. To make things even more secure, she got rid of her sister Arsinoe at the time. Arsinoe was a rebellious figure in Egypt and had more than once shown that she would like to be the one ruling the country.

It was not uncommon for all this ruthlessness to occur in the Egyptian court. Since the royals were so used to inbreeding, it was not uncommon for multiple people to feel that it was their right to be on the throne. Being only once removed from the seat of power made people jealous, and assassination was a constant worry. Cleopatra was able to effectively get rid of all major domestic threats to her throne. This enabled her to turn to actually ruling the country of Egypt and trying to keep it free.

Cleopatra at this time only had one child, and this child was not fathered by any of her brothers. This angered some in Egypt, who felt that the lineage of Egypt needed to stay pure and within the Ptolemaic family, rather than being passed down through a Roman child.

It is believed that Cleopatra was very popular and much loved by her people. Despite all of the fighting that occurred with the Roman Empire, and the fact that she and her family were not able to get along, those that she ruled adored Cleopatra, according to the few sources that are available from that time. She was able to keep Egypt free for a long time and worked to help keep the country from going broke and starving. She also turned around the way that many of her people looked at the Ptolemaic family. This family had come from Greece originally and felt that they should hold on to their Greek language and customs.

Cleopatra was determined to get on the good side of her people. She learned the Egyptian language, and she even commissioned some portraits of herself that were done in the Egyptian style. In essence, Cleopatra used some intense patriotism in order to get her people on her side and to make sure that she was able to hold onto her title as pharaoh.

This dedication to the Egyptian people was very uncommon at the time. The Ptolemy reign came from Greece. Ever since taking over Egypt, they had refused to make changes to their culture. The may have thought of themselves as gods and goddesses, like the Egyptians, but none of them claimed to be Egyptian, and none of them even knew the language. And since they married their family members, there was never really a chance of actually intermingling with the people they ruled over.

But from an early age, Cleopatra saw the value of being like the people she ruled. She chose to learn some of their customs. In addition, she started to write some of her legal documents in Egyptian, something that has helped linguists open the doors to other languages that were long thought dead. This ability to connect on a new level with her people, something that had not been done for a long time, helped Cleopatra to gain the favor of the people, win their love, and cement her place on the Egyptian throne.

Cleopatra's Rule in Summary

The rule of Cleopatra was filled with a lot of issues and strife. Cleopatra never fully controlled her own throne. She often had to share it with her father and her brothers, one of whom worked to get her exiled from her home. Even when Cleopatra did hold the reigns of the country and was a queen in her own right, she had to cozy up to the Roman Empire in the hopes of getting to keep her crown.

The story of Cleopatra's rise to the throne is just one of the many stories that helped to cement her place in history. She was beloved by her countrymen, but many times had to fear for her own life. Despite this, she was able to keep things going well for Egypt and even ensured that her son was able to rule the throne for some time after she killed herself.

Chapter 4: Cleopatra—Ruler and Queen

It took a long time before Cleopatra was able to rule her country of her own accord. She had to spend a lot of time as a co-ruler with the men in her family and was often considered a nuisance to those who thought that she should be subservient. Things came to a head when she got into a fight with her brother and was put into exile. Luckily, she was able to seduce Caesar and get her rightful place back on the throne.

But why was Cleopatra so important? Other than being the last pharaoh in Egypt and seducing two powerful men in the Roman Empire, what was she able to do that helped out her own people and made her country better? Was she able to do anything, or was she more of a figurehead that is remembered for the time and place she arose in history?

Cleopatra as Queen

Cleopatra was actually a much-loved queen of her time. The people in her country believed that she had the knowledge and experience that was needed to make them strong again and to help them out when times were getting tough. There were a few different reasons that they thought she was going to be able to help them out, including:

- She knew their language
- She knew their customs
- She had experience working with Rome
- She kept close ties with Rome during a difficult time
- She was a strong leader
- She was able to help out the economy,

which was in shambles at the time of her rule

- She changed the way marriage was viewed in her country

She knew their language and customs
Let's take a look at the first part. Cleopatra was one of the first of her line to learn the language and the customs of her country. The Ptolemaic family was not originally from Egypt. Because of this, the family had their own language and customs, and for many years, they never learned how to speak the language of those they were ruling. All the official and court documents of the time were done in Greek, paintings, plays, and other amusements were Greek, and if someone native from the country of Egypt was in the palace, they would have to learn Greek as well.
This went on for some time. Since the Ptolemaic family insisted that family members marry each other, they never got any outside influences from the country, and none of

them ever cared. But this was an issue to some of the natives of Egypt. It is difficult to imagine that the person ruling you and making all the decisions that affect your life isn't even able to speak the same language as you. While this went on for many years, there was a lot of unrest in the country by the time Cleopatra was able to take the throne.

Cleopatra was a bit different than the ancestors before her. She saw the Egyptian language and customs as important to her people, so they become important to her. She learned these things and wrote her official documents as queen in Egyptian. While this may seem like a simple thing to do, Cleopatra felt that being able to speak the language would unify her with her people and perhaps make Egypt strong enough to withstand Rome. While this may not have worked out as planned, it did gain her quite a bit of favor with her people.

Due to the fact that Cleopatra knew the language of her people at the time, some have wonder if she was born of a slave, which brought up the whole race question in the beginning. It is not likely that she had learned the Egyptian language from her family. The Ptolemaic family had been around for many years, and yet none of them had any thoughts about learning about the people they were ruling. They were happy to just be the ruling class and leave things as they were. Since none of the other Ptolemies knew Egyptian, it is unlikely Cleopatra would have learned the language from them.

The two common reasons for Cleopatra knowing and understanding the language is that either she convinced one of her tutors to teach her the language, or she had an Egyptian slave who taught her. Regardless of how Cleopatra learned this language, it served her well when she became queen and tried to win the hearts of her people.

She had experience with Rome

At this time, Rome was starting to build up its empire, and it was one of the strongest countries in the world. Most countries who tried to fight against Rome were quickly defeated and gobbled up. Only a few were able to stand free.

Egypt knew that it was in a precarious position. After many years of famine, flooding, and a poor economy brought on by internal wars, they did not stand much of a chance if Rome decided to take them over. And yet they still wanted to be a free and independent country on their own. Over the years, Ptolemy XII had worked with Rome to establish a kind of truce. Rome was interested in the waterways that led into Egypt as well as some of the land and food. Egypt pretty much offered these things to Rome, as well as a bit of allegiance, in order to remain free.

This is worked well for Cleopatra. When she was young, she had been taken to Rome and spent some time learning the customs and understanding how the Egyptian and Roman relationship went. Since Cleopatra had the right experience when it came to working with Rome, she knew how to keep the balance, and was actually able to help make

Egypt a better place through these connections.

Since Cleopatra had spent some time in Rome, she had time to learn some of the language, culture, and customs of Rome. This, perhaps more than anything else, allowed her to get along well with the Roman leaders. She knew how to talk to them, what made them tick, and how to get them to work with her better than any other Egyptian ruler.

Who else would have been able to form such close ties with the Roman Empire at that time? For the brief time that Cleopatra's brother had been around Caesar, he had almost angered the emperor so much as to start a war and sever all bonds between the two countries.

But Cleopatra did such a good job maintaining ties that she was able to get Rome to give back some of the provinces they held from years earlier. Without Cleopatra, it is certain that things would have gone downhill for Egypt much faster.

She kept close ties to Rome

Cleopatra knew early on that having a good relationship with Rome was critical if she wanted to keep her country strong and growing. Making Rome mad would result in a war that Egypt was not able to handle.

Cleopatra did this through the relationships that she founded with two of the most powerful leaders of Rome. Being a woman presented some unique challenges to helping out Rome. She couldn't fight in the army along with the men, but she had different ways to forge ties. She formed relationships both with Julius Caesar and Mark Antony which would help to keep her safe and even provide some extra territory and income for Egypt.

When it came to Julius Caesar, Cleopatra seemed interested in cementing her place as queen of Egypt and nothing else. She was happy to be mistress to Caesar and used this connection in order to be reinstated as co-ruler in Egypt. She and Caesar did end up having a child together during that time, a child that Cleopatra was able to use in several ways. First, having the first heir, one who was not born to her brother, meant that she had an even stronger position when it came to ruling her country.

Others thought she might use this birth to help connect Rome even more. If the Roman marriage laws could be changed, Cleopatra could easily become one of the wives of Caesar, and their son could then take on the throne when Caesar passed away. This would help make Rome and Egypt allies, and could do wonders for the prosperity of Egypt. This never did come about, though; the Roman laws were never changed, and Cleopatra's son was never recognized as a formal heir.

The death of Caesar was not the last tie that Cleopatra made with Rome. While it took some time to warm up to him, Cleopatra and Mark Antony soon became lovers as well, before marrying and having three children together. Antony was well respected in Rome and even ruled over a large province. Through this relationship, Cleopatra was able to get a large area of Egypt's land back, which helped her to raise revenue, lower taxes, and increase the workforce. This was a connection that Egypt was able to keep until Cleopatra died, when the county became a part of the Roman Empire.

Cleopatra was able to maintain some ties with the Roman Empire for the entirety of her life, even when things were going downhill. It wasn't until her death that the Roman Empire took over Egypt and made it one of their provinces.

She was a strong leader

Cleopatra was always thought of as a strong leader in her country. To start with, her rule began at a young age working with her father. She learned the ins and outs of running the kingdom and knew what would work best. When she and her brother became co-rulers, she took over the reins. She began to take her brother's name off of important documents and even made coins that only had her face on them. When her brother wanted to fight to get rid of her, he was drowned on the way to the battle, and she was able to keep her crown.

Even at this point, her throne was in question. The moment that Caesar died, Cleopatra knew that her throne was not as secure, and her protection was gone. Rather than waiting for someone to try and get rid of her, she chose to kill off both her brother and her sister to ensure that no one would challenge her or her son.

This strong leadership was exactly what Egypt needed at the time. Many previous leaders had not been able to keep the country unified. But Cleopatra put down rebellions swiftly. Any other leader at this time, especially with heavy Roman influence all over, would have caved. Even her first husband got in fights with Caesar that could have easily caused problems. But with her wit, charm, and good looks, Cleopatra was able to work together with the Romans and keep her country going strong.

She helped out the economy

Through her reign, Cleopatra was able to improve Egypt's economy. By the time she came to power, the economy had been trashed, and there were uprisings as a result. Cleopatra came onto the stage needing to make things better.

One of her most significant accomplishments was getting back one of the major provinces of Egypt that had been lost years before to the Romans. Her relationships with Caesar and Mark Antony helped her to get this land back. This area had some great commerce and was able to bring a lot of extra money into the country. Because of this new land, Cleopatra was able to lower taxes in other parts of the country.

This is one of the things that Egypt needed the most at the time. The Ptolemaic dynasty had been around for some time, but in general they were not strong leaders. Many of them were just there for the power and didn't have any interest in ruling. Because of interbreeding, there was never a chance for new ideas or influences.

But somehow Cleopatra was different. She took things in stride and was able to provide the strong leadership that her people were looking for, even though traditionally she should have taken a step back and let others do the work. No other members of her family would have had as much success as she did in boosting the economy and maintaining good foreign relations.

Her effect on marriage

Cleopatra had a strong effect on how marriage was seen while she was the queen. Women was expected to take a back seat to their husbands. Even as a co-ruler, Cleopatra was expected to hand the reins over to her husband and only step up when he got sick or had to leave the country for diplomatic reasons. But Cleopatra saw her job as something more than all of this. She was interested in actually running her country and refused to let her brothers take that from her. As a result, Cleopatra changed the role that women played in society. She became a symbol for strong women, something that got her into a lot of trouble with the Romans. Many women in Egypt were inspired by her. Cleopatra was held in high regard for being so strong-willed even though she had been married. Many wondered why she even followed the tradition of marrying her brothers. She certainly didn't need them around to gain the throne, and she ended up having all of her children with other men from foreign countries. But even though she was married through traditional means to her two brothers, she stood up independently and helped to steer the country in the direction it needed to go.

Her Own Family's Take on Her

Despite how much Cleopatra was loved by her own people, her family was not always that fond of her. Her father had made her co-ruler at a young age but had also limited her powers quite a bit. When her father died, Cleopatra had to share the throne with her brother, and later with another brother, rather than getting to hold onto it outright.

This did not sit well with the young queen, and she began to do even more things to anger her family. She thought she should be the one to rule. If she were male, her experience and age would dictate that she was in charge. But when she took the reins, her family became mad and put her into exile. Luckily, this did not stop Cleopatra. Think of how things would have gone for Egypt if Cleopatra had just given up when her brother exiled her? The country probably would have gone under the rule of her younger brother, who was basically under the control of his advisors. It is unlikely that Egypt would have made it on its own for much longer; remember how angry Caesar had become just spending a bit of time with the arrogant Ptolemy.

Even though Cleopatra was not well loved by her family members, and even chose to have some of them killed in order to keep her crown, she was just what the country needed at the time: a strong leader who would take chances and keep them safe, someone who would break the rules of tradition but knew when to hold it back in order to keep their allies on the right side. Cleopatra fit the bill perfectly, much better than anyone else in her family would have been able to do.

While Cleopatra is best known today for her tragic relationship with Mark Antony, she was also a powerful ruler who was able to keep Egypt free in a time of unrest, improve the economy, and become one of the best-known rulers in the world at that time.

Chapter 5: Cleopatra's Personal Relationships

The different relationships that Cleopatra had throughout her life were often a hot topic of debate. She had two legal husbands, was mistress to one of the most powerful men in the world, and had three children with another powerful Roman.

This chapter will spend some time looking at the two major relationships that Cleopatra had and how they would change the outlook that came from them.

Cleopatra's Relationship with Julius Caesar

When Cleopatra met Julius Caesar he was the leader of the Roman Empire, one of the biggest Empires in the world at that time and a major ally to Egypt, although Egypt was subservient to Rome. Before Cleopatra was been exiled by her brother and husband, the two had never met, but once they did, things began to look up for Cleopatra.

At the time, Caesar was heading to Egypt to finish a fight with his enemy Pompey. To try and save the Emperor some time and to help him get back to Rome early, Theodotus, one of the tutors of Ptolemy XIII, sailed out to meet Caesar with Pompey's head. He had hoped to gain some favor with the Emperor and get him to go home, but Caesar was furious and felt that it was a cowardly murder of his son-in-law. Based on this reaction, many felt that Caesar had never actually meant to kill Pompey, and was instead planning to show mercy, similar to what he had done for enemies in the past. Other believe that Caesar did intend to get rid of Pompey, but was angry that he was not the one who got to kill him.

Either way, this did not bode well for Ptolemy XIII. Caesar was not happy that Pompey had been killed, and he planned to execute Ptolemy in retaliation. Hearing about this plan, Ptolemy's guardians tried to stir up some anger among the people in order to scare Caesar away. This did not work, and Caesar headed to Alexandria to talk to the co-rulers. He first insisted that Cleopatra and

Ptolemy dismiss the armies, reminding them of the large debt that Egypt owed to Rome.

There are two versions of the story of how Caesar and Cleopatra met. The first one states that Cleopatra was forced to leave her home by her brother. When Cleopatra refused to go, Ptolemy was taken over with jealousy and sent her into exile. Caesar then requested to meet with them both to get a more mutual agreement. When Cleopatra was not allowed back into the castle, she sneaked in and met secretly with Caesar. Caesar was so taken by Cleopatra that he reinstated her as a co-ruler and stood by her side from that time on.

The second story shows that Ptolemy was insolent and horrible to the great Caesar. Cleopatra, trying to keep her country safe, sneaked into a secret meeting with Caesar in order to try and reverse the damage that was being done by her brother.

According to legends, Cleopatra had to be cunning in order to get an audience with Caesar. She was not welcome in the castle at that time, and if her brother and his generals had found out, she would have been turned away, or worse. Legend has it that she was rolled up into a carpet and delivered right to the emperor. While this is a fun story, most historians believe that she just veiled herself so as not to be recognized by others, and then she was able to slip in to meet the Emperor.

Once in with Caesar, Cleopatra was able to charm him. Many think that her beauty and wit won him over, while others think that he was impressed to meet someone who was a direct descendant of Ptolemy. From this first meeting, Caesar reversed the decision that Ptolemy XIII made, and ensured that Cleopatra was a co-ruler again. Soon, the two became lovers, despite both of them being married to others.

Ptolemy XIII was not happy with this turn of events. He showed up to the palace a bit later and found that Cleopatra was already there. In a fit of rage, he left the room, trying to get people to rise up against Caesar. Caesar was able to calm most of the crowds in that area by producing the will of Ptolemy XII, stating that Cleopatra was one of the heirs to the throne. While there were a few minor battles in his way to helping Cleopatra regain her right to the throne, Caesar was able to win over the area before leaving.

When Caesar went back to Rome, there were a number of things that he had to do. A lot of his critics felt that instead of fighting some small battles, Caesar should have made Egypt a part of the Roman Empire. He also had to deal with the fact that, despite Pompey being dead, there were still some factions that were loyal to him, including a few of his sons who wanted to be heirs. One important thing that Caesar did for Cleopatra was to offer her Cyprus back. With the increase in revenue from Cyprus, Cleopatra was able to reduce the taxes in other parts of the country while working to improve the poor Egyptian economy as a whole. This boded well for her popularity.

As mentioned before, Cleopatra became the lover of Caesar after meeting with him. In June of 47 B.C. she gave birth to her first son,

Ptolemy X Caesarion. Since Cleopatra was not the wife of Caesar, her son was born without any rights to the throne of Rome. Despite this, Caesar was proud that he had finally produced a male heir, and he began to consider changing Roman law so that he would be allowed to recognize this illegitimate son as an heir.

Caesar doted over his son and even invited Cleopatra and Ptolemy XIII to his villa to spend time together as family and friends. The rules of Rome were never changed, however, and Cleopatra's son was not allowed to take over the throne in Rome.

Despite Cleopatra's son not being a legitimate or formally recognized by the Romans as an heir, it was widely known that Cleopatra was the mistress of Caesar. Despite never getting to be the wife, Cleopatra was highly rewarded in society. Cleopatra was very popular with Caesar's friends and would hold many big gatherings for them. She is also considered to be responsible for bringing Mark Antony back into the favor of Caesar after a disagreement;

apparently, Antony was a big friend of the Ptolemies because he loved Greek culture and fashion just like them.

Despite the changes that Cleopatra brought to Rome during her time there and how much the nobility seemed to love her, she was not that popular with the Roman Senate. At that time, the Senate and many great thinkers felt that women should be subservient to men and should have no opinions about what was going on in the world. The women were there to please their husbands and to produce heirs, and nothing more. The outspoken and beautiful Cleopatra flew in the face of all this. She was a woman who had complete control over her country, despite having a husband as a co-ruler, held her parties, and had the ear of the most powerful man in Rome. Many people felt that this was not normal and as a result they did not like her.

Caesar was killed in 44 B.C. by a conspiracy led by Cassius and Brutus, who were worried that Caesar was becoming a tyrant. Despite some people feeling concerned about the way things were going, no one welcomed the deed of the assassins, and the conspirators were forced to flee Rome.

Once Caesar was dead, Mark Antony started to take on a more prominent role. While he was not able to do anything to the assassins, he did take care to show that he was mourning the emperor's death and he distributed Caesars will at the end.

Cleopatra was not safe for long in Rome. While some believed that she may have had a miscarriage shortly after Caesar was buried, this was never proven. While Caesar had talked with Antony about advising the Senate that he wished to make Caesarion his heir, which would have protected both Caesarion and Cleopatra, Cleopatra was sure that she was not safe. Octavian was taking over the throne based on the will that was read after Caesar died, and she knew that Octavian would not tolerate any threat to his power. Cleopatra took herself and her son back to Egypt as a result.

Cleopatra knew that she had some work to do. Up to that point, she had been safe in her position as queen thanks to the protection of Caesar. Now that he was gone, she had to cement her place on the throne. Her first husband was gone by this point, and she had followed tradition to marry her second brother. To keep things safe for her and her son, she killed off both her second brother and her only sister. This resulted in no threats to the throne from her family, and later she promoted her son co-ruler along with her.

Cleopatra's Relationship with Mark Antony

The second major relationship Cleopatra had that helped to cement the ties between Egypt and the Roman Empire, was with Mark Antony. While he was not as powerful as Caesar, the relationship had an important impact on the relations between the two countries.

Antony helped rule a part of the Roman Empire rather than all of it, but the story of Cleopatra and Mark Antony's relationship is the best remembered romance in history.

While the couple may not have been thinking all that much about romance at the time and may have just been trying to save their own skins, many people today still see the romantic side to their love and how neither could stand to live without the other.

Mark Antony was originally a general and Roman politician who worked with Julius Caesar during his reign and later became one of the biggest rivals to Octavian. While he may have met with Cleopatra a few times before Julius Caesar's death, the two did not know each other all that well, and they did not begin their romance until she had gone back to Egypt. Antony defended Cleopatra right after the death of Caesar, stating that her son was the rightful heir to the throne and that he and Cleopatra should be given safety while they were in Rome.

Mark Antony spent a lot of time in the public eye. His father had been a military commander, although he was not very good at his job, and his grandfather was an orator and consul. Antony was trained as a small boy to become a cavalry officer and he soon won important victories inside Egypt and Palestine. His mother was a cousin to Julius Caesar, which allowed him to meet the ruler and become a staff officer. Once Caesar began his dictatorship, Antony was promoted to second in command and was often at Caesar's side.

Towards the end of Caesar's life, Antony had heard that rumors of the conspiracy to kill him. He tried to get back to his friend but he was not in time. Worried that others would try to harm him in the chaos, Antony left the city of Rome disguised as a slave. Shortly after, he came back in order to protect the legacy of his friend and took over distributing Caesar's will.

After the death of Caesar, Antony quickly rouse the ire of Octavian, Caesar's successor. Octavian had been named as the one to receive the title and wealth that Caesar had left behind. Earlier in his life, before meeting Cleopatra and siring a son, Caesar had adopted his nephew as his own and declared him his son. This was most likely done in order to ensure that Caesar, who didn't have any sons at the time, would have a successful heir to follow him. It would keep the familial line going and prevent fighting over the empire when Caesar did pass on.

Antony was nervous about handing over all this power and fortune to a boy who was only 17 years old, and he made this known early on, causing the latter to become his enemy. Antony and Octavian first clashed in 43 B.C. While Octavian's army was able to push Antony back, Antony put up enough force and power that Octavian figured it was better to keep him as an ally rather than continue fighting him.

Another rival of Octavian, known as Lepidus, eventually joined with the other two, and the Second Triumvirate was formed. This group split up the provinces of Rome and protected them individually. Octavian was in charge of the western province, Antony of the eastern ones, and Lepidus got Africa. Within the next year, Antony was able to defeat the assassins of Caesar who were trying to take over parts of Rome as well; this was the battle that helped make Antony a great general.

Despite splitting up the provinces, it was understood that Octavian was the true leader. He didn't just give up his powers and treat the others like kings. Rather, they were more like noblemen who helped Octavian out. While Antony and Lepidus promised to recognize Octavian in this way, there would be issues with this concession later on for Antony.

After Caesar had died, Antony tried to get Egypt to proclaim their royalty to Rome again. He sent word to Cleopatra in order to discuss their political alliances. At the time, Cleopatra had no interest in talking to Antony, and she ended up refusing him twice before agreeing to meet for a short time.

Cleopatra was nervous about this meeting, though she had probably met Antony at some point while living in Rome. Some felt that she wanted to avoid Antony trying to turn Egypt away from Rome. Cleopatra was well aware of how close Egypt was to Rome and didn't want this to happen.

A more likely reason is that she didn't want to appear to be plotting against Octavian. Antony had once spoken out in favor of her son being the emperor. While Cleopatra had favored this plan, it did not work out well, and she had headed back home to show that she would remain peaceful. Cleopatra may have been worried that any meeting with Antony would arouse suspicion with Octavian that she was trying to place her son on the throne in his stead.

Either way, Cleopatra finally ended up meeting with Antony in Egypt. The meeting seemed to go well, and the two saw each other more frequently on different occasions as the years went on.

It wasn't until 41 B.C. that Antony began to have an affair with Cleopatra. After some time together, Antony moved back to Egypt with Cleopatra, and they were married there. The issue was that Antony had another wife. This wife, Fulvia, did not take favorably to being replaced by Cleopatra, and she decided to organize an attack against Octavian, claiming that Antony had asked her to do it. It took a long time for Antony to repair all of this damage; he started by leaving Cleopatra for awhile and going back to his wife. It was too late at this point though, as his wife died shortly afterwards.

Worried that this step would not be enough to keep him on the good side of Octavian, he choose to marry Octavia Minor, Octavian's sister, in order to reunite the two families. Unfortunately, Antony did not tell Cleopatra of any of his plans. She heard about his infidelity and how he had gone back to his wife and married another just a few weeks before giving birth to their twins. Despite this, Cleopatra continued to support Antony during his military endeavors.

While Antony was technically married to Octavia Minor, he was still in love with Cleopatra and their relationship was often flaunted in public. After this time, he had another son with Cleopatra, named Ptolemy

Philadelphus. The two lovers began to show off their relationship as well as their children, with the oldest child of Cleopatra dressed up in the costumes that royal heirs wore, despite the fact that he was illegitimate.

After some time, Antony began to worry about the intentions of Octavian and was feeling trapped in his marriage. He chose to leave Octavia Minor, who was pregnant, and go back to Cleopatra. Upset with the betrayal and how badly his sister was treated, Octavian spoke out against Cleopatra and Antony and chose to launch an attack against them. But this did not stop Antony; while he was in Egypt, he declared his loyalty and alliance with Cleopatra.

At this point, Cleopatra became scared for her life. The Roman military was strong, and she needed to be able to keep her country going despite all the fighting. She decided to hide in her personal burial tomb and start rumors that she already died. These rumors were meant to get Octavian off her trail, but while fighting, Antony heard about them as well.

Assuming that Cleopatra had actually died, he committed suicide out of grief.

Shortly after, Cleopatra heard that her husband was dead. She knew that if Octavian ever found her, she was going to be a prisoner and her life would be miserable. She chose to commit suicide as well. There are some different theories as to how Cleopatra killed herself, but most people believe that she died by having a cobra bite her.

This romantic story is the one that most people remember about Cleopatra. At a young age, only about 39, Cleopatra had been through much more than a lot of people had realized. Despite all of it, she chose to end her life after losing her one true love. Her relationship with Antony is considered the primary reason that Egypt was able to stay independent from Rome for so long. But it was also the reason that Egypt fell shortly after the death of Cleopatra.

Chapter 6: The Children of Cleopatra

During Cleopatra's life, she gave birth to four children. Interestingly enough, all of them came from Roman fathers rather than from either of her two brothers to whom she was married. The children of Cleopatra hold a lot of interest for modern historians and others who have followed Cleopatra's story. The issue is that not much of their lives was documented. Apart from Cleopatra's daughter, the children died or were killed and disappeared from the public record. This leaves a lot of uncertainty as to what happened to them.

This chapter will spend a bit of time looking at the lives of Cleopatra's four children and their impact on history.

Caesarion

The first son of Cleopatra was Ptolemy XV, although he usually went by the name of Caesarion, after his father. Caesarion was born in 47 B.C. in Egypt and spent a lot of his early life in Rome as a guest of Caesar. Cleopatra had hopes that her son would be the ruler of Rome once Caesar died. This would bring together the kingdoms of Egypt and Rome, as Caesarion would be the rightful heir to both.

Caesar actually worked to see if it was possible to change the laws of the land. He had never produced a male heir until Caesarion was born. It was legal for Caesar to have more than one wife, but Roman law didn't allow for the wife to be foreign-born. This excluded Caesar from marrying Cleopatra and making Caesarion his rightful heir. Caesar tried to change this law, but since many in the Senate didn't like Cleopatra, it was difficult for Caesar to make any progress.

When Caesar was assassinated a few years later, Cleopatra returned to Egypt with her son and later made him a co-ruler along with herself. This was basically just a royal title for her son, since Cleopatra kept the power to herself.

Historically, Caesarion was more a minor figure. While his mother portrayed him as the child Horus to her Isis, he had no real power.

Cleopatra may have trained him to eventually take over the throne once she passed on, but she kept most of the power to herself.

For the next few years, there isn't much recorded about Caesarion at all. He finally reappears in some historical texts in 36 and 34 B.C. during the Donations of Antioch. Both of these donations were held by Antony and Cleopatra as a ceremony that allowed Cleopatra's children to regain lands that had been taken over by Rome. This showed that Rome wanted to be friends with Egypt and keep them as allies.

These were not just acts of rebellion on Antony's part, though; Octavian was notified of the donations and gave his approval. Antony soon became bolder with his choices. He had a huge party and started parading all four children around as if they were the rulers of the land. During this time, Antony declared Caesarion a god and a king of kings and even went so far as to describe him as the sole heir of Caesar and ruler of all of Rome.

This started to cause problems. Octavian considered himself the one and only heir to the Roman throne. Calling Caesarion the direct heir was a threat to Octavian.

During most of his life, Caesarion was being groomed in order to take over the throne for his mother. She had written in her will that Caesarion was going to be the sole ruler once she passed. Some believe that Cleopatra knew that she would need to hide and go into exile with Antony to escape Octavian, and she was getting her son ready to take over near the end of her life.

When Cleopatra died, the throne of Egypt fell to Caesarion for a bit of time. Egypt did not last long as an independent kingdom; Caesarion only ruled for as long as it took Octavian to find him. In August of 30 B.C., Octavian conquered the capital of Egypt and the empire became a part of Rome. How Caesarion died is unsure. Some believe that Octavian executed him right in Alexandria, while some thought that he was strangled. Some believed that he went into hiding, came up with a new identity, and died at an old age. But the exact circumstances that surround his death are not documented, so it is all speculation.

Once Caesarion was killed, Octavian was able to take total control of Egypt. Because Caesarion wasn't a ruler for very long, his mother Cleopatra is still considered the last ruler in Egypt before the Roman Empire took over.

Caesarion is the child of whose early years the most is known about, but because he was the first to be killed after his mothers' death, and because very little was written about him in his childhood, most of the details of his life are unknown.

Alexander Helios

The second child of Cleopatra was Alexander Helios. He and his twin sister were the first heirs to Cleopatra and Mark Antony. While he was never able to hold any power in Egypt, he was still an important figure in helping to bring together Egypt and Rome.

Apart from being the son of Mark Antony and Cleopatra, not too much is known about Alexander. Even the exact date of his death is unknown as no one was paying that much attention after his mother and father had passed. His fraternal twin was named Cleopatra Selene II. They were half Roman, half Macedonian Greek, adding in a little diversity to the Ptolemaic dynasty that had been inbreeding for years.

It is believed that Cleopatra named this son after their collateral ancestor, Alexander the Great, in order to show some of the history of the Egyptian line. Alexander's second name meant "the sun" in ancient Greek. This is the counterpart to the second name of his twin sister, Selene, which means "the moon".

Alexander is believed to have been born, raised, and educated in Alexandria. He was the second out of Cleopatra's three sons. During the Donations of Alexandria, Alexander was given the same title of King of Kings as his older brother, and he gained the title of ruler over some parts of Egypt. For

Alexander, the ruling areas including Parthia, Media, and Armenia, as well as countries that have not been discovered between the Indus and Euphrates Rivers. This was in spite of the fact that this territory wasn't even in the control of Antony and Cleopatra at the time.

There is some record that Alexander was engaged to be married to Iotapa, a woman who was distantly related to him and was the Princess of Media Atropatene. This would have helped to cement the title that his father and mother had already given him in terms of which lands he would rule. But this relationship never came to be. Alexander's fate changed after this ceremony and after both his parents committed suicide in order to escape Octavian.

After Antony and Cleopatra committed suicide, Alexander was spared, along with his sister and his younger brother. The story goes that when Octavian returned triumphant to Rome, he paraded these children around the streets wearing golden chains, following a small statue of their mother holding the asp to her arm. It is believed that Ptolemy Philadelphus, the younger brother of Alexander, would have made the journey as well, but some believe that he may have perished on the journey from Egypt to Rome due to the fact that he is not mentioned in historical records after this point.

After this parade, the children were treated pretty well. Alexander and his siblings were given to Octavia Minor, the sister of Octavian and one of the wives of Mark Antony. She took them in and raised them. Octavia educated and raised them alongside her own children.

What happened to Alexander Helios is uncertain, and the exact date of his death is still unknown. It is believed that Alexander was spared at his sister's request after she married King Juba II, but some believe this is just legend. In all probability, Alexander lived peacefully in Rome to an old age.

While many believed that Cleopatra was just with Caesar for convenience and to ensure her power in Egypt and possibly in Rome, it is believed that Cleopatra was with Antony for love. There wasn't any reason that she needed to marry again. She already had married twice and produced an heir from her lover. He had killed off anyone that had tried to take over her throne, and she probably would have been able to keep Egypt free if she had ignored Antony and maintained her allegiance to Octavian.

Despite this, Cleopatra chose to meet with and eventually marry Antony. Alexander Helios and his sister are the results of that love. And while her first son disappeared shortly after Octavian captured Egypt, it is believed that Octavian had enough respect for all that Cleopatra had done to make sure that this oldest living son, as well as his siblings, were given a proper life and education.

Cleopatra Selene II

A little bit more is known about the one and only daughter of Cleopatra, Cleopatra Selene II. While her brothers were potential threats to Octavian in terms of going after the throne,

Selene was seen as a potential ally to Rome, and Octavian favored her greatly and found a suitable match for her to marry.

Selene was the fraternal twin of Alexander Helios. She also had a younger brother and an older step-brother. She lived and grew up in Alexandria until her parents committed suicide during the siege of Octavian. Afterwards, she was spared by Octavian and sent to live in Rome. While the defeat parade was embarrassing and caused some harm to her pride, she was treated very well there. She still received her education and was raised in Roman society by Octavia.

As Selene grew older, it was time for her to get married. Octavian planned to use her in order to forge new alliances with the countries around him. Sometime between 26 and 20 B.C., Octavian decided to marry Selene to King Juba II of Numidia. In order to help make the match work, Octavian offered up a huge dowry as a wedding. By that time, her two brothers had disappeared from all of the historical records. Most assume the two died through assassination or from some kind of illness.

This means that at the time of her marriage, Selene was the last living member of the Ptolemaic dynasty. Once Selene was married to Juba, they were not allowed to go back to Numidia, since it had become part of the Roman Empire in 46 B.C. Instead of going back to Juba's homeland, the two were sent off to Mauretania, a territory that was unorganized and in need of supervision from Rome. In honor of their new emperor, they decided to name the capital Caesarea.

The couple was able to work wonders in the new province, and they worked really well together. Juba had experience with making policies and running a country, but Selene was able to exercise her influence and experience to determine which polices were chosen. With the influence of Selene, the kingdom flourished in trade and exports with other countries throughout the Mediterranean.

Juba and Selene had two children. The first one was born in 10 B.C., and they named him Ptolemy of Mauretania, in honor of his ancestors from the Ptolemaic dynasty. There are also some records that indicate the birth of an unnamed daughter who might have been Drusilla of Mauretania, though some speculate she was their granddaughter. She is referred to as the granddaughter of Cleopatra and Antony and as the daughter of Ptolemy of Mauretania.

A lot of controversy surrounds Selene's death, and many aren't even sure of the exact date. In 17 A.D., coins were minted with Selene's image, suggesting that she was alive for longer than originally thought. Many believed that Juba had married a Cappadocian princess but that he married her after Selene had died. If Selene was able to mint these coins, however, Juba would have married the princess while Selene was still alive.

Some historians believe that Juba and Selene had some sort of rift, which was eventually fixed once Juba divorced the princess. In most cases, historians don't believe that Juba would have taken on two wives, even though he was Romanized. The most common argument is that if he had married the princess before 4 A.D., then Selene must have been dead, although some believe that the princess might have been a second wife.

While the date of Selene's death is uncertain, when she did die, she was laid to rest in the Royal Mausoleum in Mauretania, which is in Algeria.

Selene was probably the most well-known and prosperous of the children of Cleopatra. She was allowed to work with Octavian for the good of the Roman Empire. Of course, he could not allow her to rule her native country of Egypt, despite the fact that Egypt was now a province of Rome. It would have been too easy for the natives of that country to rally behind her and start up a revolution.

But Octavian must have seen that keeping the daughter of Cleopatra on his side could help him. He married her off to a nobleman and allowed them to help rule a province, although it was quite a distance away from Egypt. The two were well-loved in the area, and still today you can find buildings and statues there that were made in their honor. This shows that they were respected rulers.

Ptolemy Philadelphus

Ptolemy Philadelphus was the youngest son of Cleopatra and Mark Antony. Like his older brother and sister, he had Roman and Greek heritage. He would have been considered fourth in line to the Egyptian throne if the country had remained free, and no other heirs had been produced. Unlike his older two siblings, Ptolemy was born in Antioch Syria, which would be in modern day Turkey. While the name of Ptolemy was common in Cleopatra's family, she named her son after Ptolemy II Philadelphus, the second pharaoh to rule in the Ptolemaic dynasty. Many believe that Cleopatra chose this name for her son in order to try and recreate the Ptolemaic kingdom in all its glory.

Ptolemy's brothers were not the only ones who were given gifts during the Donations of

Alexandria. During this celebration, Ptolemy was also recognized and named the ruler of Cilicia, Phoenicia, and Syria. After the death of his parents through suicide, Ptolemy was forced to go back to Rome with Octavian and had to parade around in heavy chains in the streets along with his siblings. Luckily, once this was over, he and his siblings were welcomed into the home of Octavia Minor and given a good life and education.

After this time, the fate of the youngest child of Cleopatra is unknown. It is not believed that he was killed, since there are no records of this, and most believe that the only son of Antony's that was killed by Octavian is Marcus Antonius Antyllus. In addition, there are no sources that mention a political career or military service for the young man. Scandals, marriage plans, and descendants were never discussed either. It isn't even known if Ptolemy made it into adulthood. It is commonly believed that Ptolemy died sometime during the winter of 29 B.C.

Being the youngest of Cleopatra's children, he occasioned little interest in his life. He is remembered for nothing else but being a son of Cleopatra and Antony.

While their histories are all brief, the children of Cleopatra all played a role in history. Many find it interesting that the only one Octavian killed and tortured was Caesarion, the one who had power. The rest were able to live with his own sister and were given places in society. In the case of Cleopatra's daughter, Octavian arranged her marriage, gave her a large dowry, and allowed her and her husband to rule over a part of the Roman Empire. Perhaps Octavian felt some remorse at how things ended with Antony and Cleopatra. He may have just felt that the younger three children held no threat to his own power, and so he let them live.

Chapter 7: Cleopatra and the Roman War

Octavian was worried that Antony and Cleopatra were jeopardizing his right to rule Rome. They had flaunted their power and publicly stated that Cleopatra's son, Caesarion, should be the ruler of the Roman Empire. After some time, Octavian got tired of this, and one of the Roman civil wars, known as the Battle of Actium, began in 31 B.C. as a result.

Even though Antony and Octavian had fought some small battles together, Octavian never fully trusted Antony. Antony offered to marry the sister of Octavian in order to make peace. But this backfired when Antony left her for Cleopatra. Octavian had accepted the marriage offer as a way to make peace, and instead Antony divorced her and left her to fend for herself while pregnant.

Instead of taking a step back and asking for mercy from Octavian, which surely would have helped their cause, Antony and Cleopatra continued to promote their children as the true heirs of the Roman

Empire. Many assume that Mark Antony was not ready to fight a war. They thought that he was bluffing, that there was no way that he would be able to fight off Octavian, the ruler of the Roman Empire. These people had forgotten that Antony had the allegiance of many Romans. He also had Cleopatra. This helped to make him a more even match for Octavian.

Octavian had about 19,000 men willing to fight for him, and about 400 ships. While Antony had only about 290 ships, he had more than 22,000 men willing to fight.

The Overview

Once Caesar was killed in 44 B.C., Octavian decided to create the Second Triumvirate with Lepidus and Antony. Together they kept down any uprisings against Octavian and crushed the conspirators who were guilty of Caesar's death. After this was all done, the Roman Empire was split up amongst the three. Octavian was in charge of the western provinces. Antony, as his right-hand man, was given the east, and Lepidus got North Africa.

The ties between Octavian and Antony were not always strong. Octavian was worried that Antony would try to take over the throne, because Antony had lobbied to make Cleopatra's son Emperor. In 40 B.C., Antony married Octavia, sister of Octavian, in an effort to mend their relationship. While this appeased Octavian for a time, he remained suspicious of Antony and spread propaganda to lessen his popularity.

Things began to go sour again in 37 BC. Antony married Cleopatra, even though he was still married to Octavia. He rewarded her with large grants of land for her children, expanded his power the east, and ultimately divorced Octavia publicly while she was pregnant in 32 B.C.

Octavian responded by announcing that he had read Antony's will, which supposedly affirmed that Caesarion, the oldest son to Cleopatra, was the true heir of the Roman Empire. Antony had also promised legacies to all of Cleopatra's children, even though this wasn't allowed under Roman Law. Finally,

Antony had also requested that he be buried in Alexandria right by Cleopatra, when he died.

The point of this was to make the citizens of Rome upset with Antony, and it worked. They began to think that Antony was trying to make Cleopatra the new ruler of Rome, and they didn't want a foreigner ruling their country. Octavian used this as a way to start war against Antony, while Antony and Cleopatra decided to wait in order to get some more troops from one of their loyal kings.

Octavian was not known as a great general. He was able to do the job, but he recognized his weaknesses early. Because of this, Octavian chose to have Marcus Agrippa, one of his friends, take over. Agrippa was a skilled veteran who started aggressive tactics by raiding the coast of Greece, while Octavian started to take his army to the east. Antony's fleet, on the other hand, gathered in Actium, in the Gulf of Ambracia.

While Antony was in the port, Agrippa began to attack in Messenia, damaging supply lines. Meanwhile, Octavian arrived near Actium as well and headed for the higher ground in the north.

Antony was able to hold his own during this time, and a stalemate occurred for the next few months. Both sides were wary and waited to see who would make the first move. The tides turned when Agrippa blockaded Antony and his troops, leaving them without supplies, and many of his officers started defecting.

Antony was starting to run out of options. He didn't want to stick around to see how many of his men would disappear, and he was also longing to get back to his home and wife. Nonetheless, he stayed with his troops and began to fight in 31 B.C.

Antony started with his fleet. His ships were large and formidable, but they were also slow and really hard to move around. When Octavian saw that Antony was trying to leave the harbor, he sent Agrippa out with their fleets, which had smaller boats that were easy to maneuver. Agrippa's fleet might not be as powerful as Antony's, but they wouldn't be harmed through a ramming attack.

The battle raged on. Agrippa, hoping to turn the right flank of Antony's fleet, started to extend his left. In order to respond to this attack, the right wing of Antony's fleet began to shift outwards. This did not go as planned since the right wing started detaching from the center of the fleet, leaving a gap. Agrippa noticed this opportunity quickly and plunged in.

This battle was unique because ramming was not possible. The boats on Agrippa's side were too small to do this, and they were fast enough to get away before Antony's ships could ram into them. This made battle difficult, since ramming was the normal method for fighting on the sea. The fighting ensued for the next few hours, each side taking a turn fighting and then retreating.

Cleopatra and her Egyptian ships were in the rear. Cleopatra didn't want to send her men to die for no reason. She decided that the battle was over, and she told her sixty ships to head out to sea and start for home. When the Egyptians left, the lines of Antony's fleet were placed out of order, and things started to go downhill.

Antony was stunned by this departure and decided to go after his wife with another forty ships. This meant that Antony's fleet was all of a sudden down by 100 ships, and they were now doomed to fail. There were some that valiantly fought on against Octavian; most decided that the cause was lost and started to leave the area. By that afternoon, the few ships that were left fighting agreed to surrender to Agrippa.

Antony was able to catch up to Cleopatra during her escape and get on board with her. He was angry at first with his wife, but soon they were reconciled, and the two went off to Egypt. Several of Octavian's ships tried the follow the pair, but they were able to make it all the way to Egypt unharmed.

There are a lot of theories as to why Cleopatra decided to leave. The most common one is that she saw how badly the war was going. Rather than risk losing all of her ships, she decided to spare her men. This seems the most probable explanation, since Antony left shortly after her departure, and the two went to Egypt together.

On the other hand, some wonder if she wanted her lover to be harmed. Antony was not losing at that point, but the fact that she took away 60 ships from his lines made it pretty easy for Octavian to win. Why would Cleopatra let this happen? Could she have had some sort of agreement with Octavian? It seems strange to many that Cleopatra would run away the last minute.

Either way, Cleopatra has been criticized for how she reacted at the end of this battle. She was supposed to be there in order to support Antony. She was part of the flank, and once she was gone, most knew that the war was over. While they might not have beaten Octavian anyway, there was no chance once a big percentage of their forces disappeared.

Why Cleopatra chose to run is unknown, but it pretty much spelled her doom.

What Happened After the Battle

Figuring out exactly how many people died during this battle is difficult. Numbers were not kept as well as they are today, and most tallies were just estimates. It is guessed that Octavian saw losses of about 2500 men, and that Antony lost 5000 men and 200 ships that were either captured or sunk.

When Antony was defeated, the impact was far-reaching. Antony started to lose his allies as they deserted him.

In the end, Antony killed himself, and Octavian also ended up killing Cleopatra's son, Caesarion, thus getting rid of all the blockades in the way of him becoming supreme ruler in Rome.

Chapter 8: The Death of Cleopatra

The story of Cleopatra's death has been recorded in plays and movies over the centuries. It is difficult to know which one is the truth. The Romans, the Egyptians, and those who knew Cleopatra the best, all have different versions. In this chapter, we will take a look at the different stories that are told about Cleopatra's death and try to determine which one is correct.

Cleopatra's death is one of the biggest reasons that people remember who she was. Even before studying her in school or reading this book to learn more, most people have an idea of who this queen is. But most of them don't know about her great accomplishments as queen. Rather, they know about her relationships with Julius Caesar and Mark Antony, and they know about her tragic death when she found out that Antony had killed himself.

Everyone has seen the stories, the plays, and the movies that portray this tragic ending.

But each of these stories takes on a different version of the story. Some claim that Cleopatra found out about the death of her lover and killed herself. Others felt that she decided to commit suicide in order to avoid being captured and tortured by Octavian. Still others think that Octavian found Cleopatra in hiding and killed her himself.

The one thing that is known for certain about the death of Cleopatra is that she committed suicide by hold an asp to her arm until it bit her. This bite was poisonous enough that she died pretty quickly. An asp is an old word for a type of snake that is common in Egypt. Cleopatra knew that her death would be quick.

Some people wonder why Cleopatra killed herself. Wouldn't it have been better for her to come out of hiding, especially once her lover was dead, go back to her throne, and then order her army to fight off Rome?

Basically, Cleopatra knew that everything was hopeless. Her army was not ready to fight off the powerful Roman army on its own.

Remember that out of 300 ships that fought against Octavian, Cleopatra only offered 60, and she had retreated as soon as things looked bleak. Plus she knew that most of the allies Antony had gathered had fled after the tide of the battle turned. There was no way that Cleopatra was going to win. The best she could hope for wat that Octavian would deal kindly with her children.

The evidence of Cleopatra having been bitten by an asp is found in the documents of Strabo. This writer lived in Alexandria at the time of Cleopatra's death. He knew there would be multiple versions of the story of Cleopatra's death, and that no one besides Cleopatra could know which one was true.

To start with, there are two ways that Cleopatra might have committed suicide. The fact that she killed herself is not in question; most people don't believe that Octavian was the one to kill her. If Octavian had found Cleopatra alive, he would have paraded her through the streets of Rome in chains just like he did to her children. Since this never happened, most assume that she killed herself, or had one of her servants do it.

The first idea is that Cleopatra was able to kill herself with some kind of ointment. Cleopatra might have been worried that at some point she would need to kill herself in order to prevent capture. She had spit in the face of Octavian far too often to avoid retribution. She may also have carried the poisoned ointment with her just in case. She did not hesitate to kill anyone who got in her way; she killed her own brothers and sister to keep her throne. Knowing this, it is not that strange to think she may have kept a means of ending her life swiftly on her person, to give as a gift or to use as a weapon. She probably had a slave or servant who was able to make the ointment for her.

The more popular version of the story is the one where she found the asp and held it to her arms or breast until it bit her. Asps were common in Alexanderia, and they lived in the tombs where she was hiding from Octavian, so it wouldn't have been hard to get ahold of one. Many poets and even historians who write about this era talk about how Cleopatra used two asps in order to ensure that the venom took and that she would die immediately. In most of the paintings that depict the death of Cleopatra, she is depicted with the asps. Death by asp bite was considered a noble way for her to go; it ensured that she would be sent to the spirit world as a goddess like she was on earth.

There are some who think that neither of these two versions of her death make sense. While the theories that Octavian killed the queen are still considered unlikely, some assume that other poisons were used. In fact, Christophe Schaefer, a German historian, believes that Cleopatra consumed a mixture of wolfsbane, opium, and hemlock. The reasoning for this is that most people believe that Cleopatra's death was slow and not too painful. If she had died from the asp bite, her death would have been very painful.

In Plutarch's version of the story, Octavian found Cleopatra and captured her once

Antony died. It was Octavian's plan to take Cleopatra back to Rome and present her to the public. Octavian had his servants watch over her to make sure that she didn't escape or try to harm herself before they could get back to Rome.

Despite these precautions, Cleopatra was able to find an asp, which was hiding in a basket of figs. She had this asp give her a deadly bite on the hand. The biggest issue with this story is that Plutarch was not around until 130 years after Cleopatra had passed. This means he wasn't there at the time and was going on old texts and guesswork. While he may be right, the further you get from the historical event, the less accurate a report is likely to be.

The story that is the most popular, and which is shown in literature and film, is slightly different. This version is a bit more romanticized and shows Cleopatra as a strong woman who would do anything to be with her lover.

In this version, Antony and Cleopatra had become separated after they lost the battle with Octavian. Antony had gone in one direction in order to try and keep his allies and regroup, while Cleopatra went back to Alexandria to be with her people and regroup as well.

The exact reason for Antony and Cleopatra becoming separated is not well-known. Some believe that Antony needed to rally his troops while Cleopatra needed to go back to her country and reorganize. Others believe this may have been a way to confuse Octavian. Being separated would make it would harder to find them, and give them a better chance of surviving. Later, they might have planned to meet at some predetermined spot and then flee far away from Rome together.

Cleopatra knew that she wouldn't be able to take over the throne again as queen. Luckily, she had already worked to train her son to take over Egypt. Cleopatra knew that the only way she would be able to escape was if Octavian thought she was dead, so she went into her prepared tomb with enough food and water to spend some time down there. She started to spread the rumor that she had died and made funeral preparations.

The problem came when Antony heard the rumors. While Cleopatra had been worried about getting the news to Octavian, she didn't take care to let Antony know about the plan. Before anyone could tell Antony she was alive, he stabbed himself to death in order to be with his love.

Soon word got back to Cleopatra that her lover had killed himself. She was devastated. She also knew that Octavian was going to find her. Cleopatra decided that it was time to die as well, rather than let Octavian win. Cleopatra then either found an asp in the tomb or asked someone to bring the asp to her.

This is one of the places where historians disagree. Some thought that she had stabbed herself, while others liked the asp story, and still others said that she took a deadly mix of poisons. Regardless of the method, Octavian found her lying dead in her own tomb, and had to settle for taking her sons and daughter back to Rome. No matter which story you believe, it is still a story of bravery and love.

Chapter 9: The Timeline of Major Events in Cleopatra's Life

Understanding everything that went on during Cleopatra's lifetime is difficult. She was a big figure on the world stage and the events that took place during her lifetime are amazing. Most monarchs oversee one or two major events, but Cleopatra spent a lot of her life fighting for the crown, keeping the Romans happy, and trying to run a country.

Many historians have difficulty figuring out the exact timeline of Cleopatra's life or even how old she was when she took power, or when she died. Here is a timeline of all the things that happened in Cleopatra's life. It demonstrates how amazing she truly was and why she has inspired so much thought and devotion throughout the years.

69 B.C.

This is the year that Cleopatra is born in the palace of Alexandria. She is the first daughter of Ptolemy XII. Her mother's identity is unknown, but she is believed to be one of the Cleopatras of the Ptolemaic family.

Not too much is known about the early years of Cleopatra. She is one of the favorites of her father and spends some time in the Roman Empire with him in order to forge ties. Cleopatra is named as co-ruler along with her father when they return from their trip to Rome.

Despite being one of the co-rulers of Egypt, Cleopatra doesn't have a lot of power. While her father may have been training her to help take over the country at some point, she is still a woman and is expected to be subordinate to him. She learns a lot about the country and how to rule it, but her power is mostly symbolic.

When it comes time for her to rule along with her brother, she is able to stop some rebellions and fix some of the social issues that have plagued the country for years that even her father wasn't able to handle. Thanks to this, she becomes a powerful leader, the type of leader that Egypt really needed at the time.

51 B.C.

Ptolemy Auletes, Cleopatra's father, dies. He leaves his daughter, who is just 18 years old, in charge of the kingdom, along with her brother, who is only ten. Cleopatra and her young brother get married, as is the tradition among the Ptolemaic family to keep the line pure. She had worked along with her father for about 4 years before he died.

In the beginning, things go smoothly. Cleopatra's brother, Ptolemy XIII, is under the guidance of his sister. She is able to sign legal documents and run the government. As the years go on, however, Ptolemy starts to expect his sister to relinquish some of her control to him.

Instead, Cleopatra continues to distance herself from her brother and amass power for herself. While this is fine with her people, it angers her younger brother.

48 B.C.

By this time, Cleopatra has begun to feel that the throne is rightly hers. She begins to sign legal documents without her husband and without his name, and put her own face on coins. This angers her brother which starts a huge family feud.

In 48 B.C., Cleopatra is removed from power by her brother. She is exiled from the palace. It is uncertain whether Ptolemy himself exiles his sister out of jealousy, or whether his power-hungry advisors, who are interested in keeping the rule to themselves, make this happen. Either way, Cleopatra is forced to leave her home.

During this year, Caesar comes to Alexandria to mediate between Cleopatra and Ptolemy, but Ptolemy refuses to let Cleopatra attend the negotiations. Cleopatra sneaks into the place to meet Caesar and ends up winning him to her side. There are several versions of the story of how she gets in to see Caesar; some believe that she was rolled up into a rug, others believe that she was just disguised. After a battle, Ptolemy is killed during a flood on the Nile, and Cleopatra is given the throne back after marrying her second brother.

47 B.C.

During this year, it is discovered that Caesar and Cleopatra have been having an affair. Their son is born on June 23. They name him Ptolemy Caesar, or Caesarion. This helps Cleopatra to cement herself on the throne, at least as long as Caesar is around and willing to help her to stay there.

Cleopatra spends the next few years in Rome. Caesar is happy to finally have a son to call his own. While Caesar has an adopted son, he starts to regard Caesarion as his one true heir. This son is not formally recognized in Rome, since Cleopatra is a foreigner. Despite this, Caesar and Cleopatra remain together in Rome, raising their son, until Caesar is killed a few years later.

44 B.C.

Caesar is killed in Rome in March of this year. There is a lot of unrest regarding who should take the throne next, and Cleopatra knows that she might not be welcome or safe in the Roman Empire for much longer, so she flees back to Alexandria.

Octavian, nephew and adopted son of Caesar, claims his rightful place as emperor. He is a young boy of only 17 at the time, and many fear that he won't be able to handle the complexities of ruling such a large empire. Many oppose him, but Octavian holds onto power.

During this time, Antony speaks out on Cleopatra's behalf. He feels that Cleopatra should be allowed to remain safely in Rome, as she is the mother of Caesar's biological son. But the Roman laws regarding succession do not change. Despite barely knowing Cleopatra, Antony makes enemies by defending her, and is nearly exiled.

Luckily, he is able to save face a bit after Cleopatra leaves the city. He fights Octavian in a small war, which he loses, but they become after. To cement the deal, Antony agrees to marry Octavia, the sister of Octavian.

When Cleopatra gets home, she reportedly kills her brother and husband, as well as her sister, in order to prevent anyone from trying to overthrow her.

41 B.C.

During this year, Cleopatra meets Mark Antony at Tarsus and he follows her to Egypt. They end up having three children together; a set of twins and another son later on.

The relationship between Cleopatra and Antony is tumultuous. Antony is first married to another woman, Fulvia, who becomes jealous about Cleopatra. In revenge for being deserted, Fulvia sets up a plot to kill Octavian and blames it all on Antony. After Fulvia's death, to save himself, Antony marries Octavia, the sister of Octavian. Soon after, he returns to Cleopatra and their children in Egypt. The two are together over the next few years.

32 B.C.

Antony formally divorces Octavia during this year. Octavian is not happy that his sister, who is pregnant with Antony's child, is being dumped so unceremoniously. He figures that Cleopatra and Antony have plans to team up and depose him, using Caesarion as a figurehead.

The western provinces ruled by Octavian declare war on Cleopatra. This dissolves Egypt's ties to Rome.

31 B.C.

The Battle of Actium takes place in September. Octavian is the victor, which forces Cleopatra and Antony to flee to safety in Alexandria. Just one year later, Octavian's forces arrive in the city.

30 B.C.

Antony and Cleopatra are losing men on all sides. They know it is only a matter of time before Octavian captures them. Antony decides to commit suicide in order to avoid the torture and defeat. According to tradition, Cleopatra kills herself as well.

It is believed that Antony kills himself using a spear after hearing rumors that Cleopatra is dead. Once Antony has committed suicide, he is brought to Cleopatra, who is so burdened by grief and worry about being a prisoner of decides to commit suicide as well. The exact way Cleopatra died is uncertain, but most historians believe that she dies from a self-inflicted cobra bite.

After the deaths of both Antony and Cleopatra, the fate of Egypt is sealed. Even though Caesarion, Cleopatra's first son, tries to rule Egypt for a time, Octavian soon deposes and kills him. Egypt becomes one of the new provinces of the Roman Empire.

These are just a few of the events that occurred during Cleopatra's lifetime. In the end, she never made it to her 40th birthday.

Chapter 10: Cleopatra Through the Years—

Popular Portrayals of the Royal Queen

Cleopatra was a woman like no other. She lived during a time when women stayed quietly in the background. That is not to say that women didn't have a hand in influencing history, but none held the same presence on the world stage during the time of the Roman Empire as Cleopatra.

But what is really amazing now is all of the ways that Cleopatra is remembered. While most other monarchs, even if they are well-known, are only talked about during their own time, Cleopatra still finds a way to stun and awe audiences over 2000 years after she died. It is possible to find Cleopatra almost every where that you look, including on television and film, and in literature and art.

There are not many historical figures who have been portrayed as often as this young woman has. For someone who didn't even make it to her 40's, it is amazing to see how much people still revere her and love her story.

This chapter is going to take a look at different portrayals of Cleopatra through the years.

Cleopatra in Literature

This examination of Cleopatra in literature is not going to include biographies and historical books. Rather, these are works of fiction that still place Cleopatra right in the context of cultural and historical events. Some of the works that Cleopatra is featured in include:

Cleopatra, by Jules-Emile-Fredric Massenet

This is an opera consisting of four acts. It didn't open until almost two years following the death of the composer. This opera focuses on the love story between Cleopatra and Mark Antony, one of the best known stories about the young queen. In this opera, Mark Antony comes to meet Cleopatra for the first time only after he has conquered all of Egypt. He becomes obsessed with her beauty, and, giving up all of the obligations that he has in Rome, returns to Egypt with Cleopatra. But not everything is happy for the two lovers. Antony spends some time back in

Rome in order to fulfil a promise to be married to Octavia, but he lusts after Cleopatra so much that he returns.

The play ends with a tragic love scene where Antony and Cleopatra, each believing the other is dead, kill themselves to be reunited at a different time and place.

This opera was well-received. It began performances in 1914 and had its first opening in America in 1916. There were still various performances of this opera going on as of 2012.

William Shakespeare's *Antony and Cleopatra*

This is probably the most well-known adaptation of the story of Cleopatra. Shakespeare's play follows the love triangle between Cleopatra and her two lovers. While there is no evidence that Cleopatra was with Antony during her time with Caesar, the play takes some liberties and says that she loved them both. The play goes on to show how both men know of her love for the other and for themselves; any time one of them fails, they assume that Cleopatra is the one who tricked them and is to blame.

In the end, Antony decides that he can no longer trust Cleopatra and plans to have her killed. Then he hears that she has already died, and in grief, he stabs himself with his own sword. He is then carried to the feet of his lover, where he dies. Cleopatra kills herself in turn by holding the fabled asps to her arm.

While this play takes some liberties with the story, the love triangle makes the story more relatable.

H. Rider Haggard's *Cleopatra*

This author takes a slightly different approach to the Cleopatra story. The story is told from the point of view of Harmachis, an Egyptian priest, who finds some papyrus scrolls in a tomb that tell the story of Cleopatra. The language is biblical and portrays Cleopatra with all her presence, treachery, and wit.

George Bernard Shaw's *Caesar and Cleopatra*

George Bernard Shaw's 1898, about Cleopatra and Julius Caesar was first performed in 1901. Beginning with a prologue in which the gods talk to the audience, this play depicts the first meeting of Cleopatra and Caesar. There are some creative licenses taken with the story, such as Caesar meeting Cleopatra underneath a sphinx and falling in love with her before she knew who he was. But overall, it does a great job of explaining how Cleopatra got her throne back, how the two got together.

Margaret George—*The Memoirs of Cleopatra*

This story is a little bit unique in that it is told by Cleopatra herself. It starts off when Cleopatra is about 20 years old and talks about her meeting Caesar and trying to seduce him, and it goes on until her death with Mark Antony. It is fiction, but includes a lot of historical data. While there are a lot of stories about the queen and most of them tell a romantic or sexual story, this one focuses more on the historical background.

Cleopatra in Paintings

Cleopatra has also been the subject of many famous paintings. The most famous one doesn't exist any more. It was commissioned by Octavian and is supposed to have shown

Cleopatra being paraded through the streets in chains. This portrait was engraved during the nineteenth century and became part of someone's private collection in Sorrento. Since that time, the painting has been lost and no one is sure where it ended up. Some assume that the painting was never done in the first place or that it was destroyed during the fall of the Roman Empire.

Some of the other best known paintings include:

- *Suicide of Cleopatra*—This was a painting of Giovanni Barbieri and was done in 1631. It is an oil painting and is currently in Pasadena, California in the Norton Simon Museum. This painting shows Cleopatra holding the snake right before her death.
- *The Banquet of Cleopatra*—This is an oil painting that was done in 1743 by Giambattista Tiepolo. It can be found in Victoria, Australia in their National Gallery. It shows a famous banquet where it is said Cleopatra used a glass of vinegar to dissolve a pearl earring.

- *Cleopatra and the Peasant*—This painting was done by Eugene Delacroix in 1838. It is found at the University of North Carolina in the Ackland Art Museum. This painting shows a man handing over the snake that Cleopatra will use in order to kill herself.
- *Cleopatra and Caesar*—This painting was done in 1866 by Jean-Leon Gerome. There are now only copies of this painting, as the original was lost. This painting shows Caesar sitting on his throne while Cleopatra stands before him. It is painted in an eastern style.
- *The Death of Cleopatra*—Jean Andre Rixens was the artist for this painting, which was done in 1874. You can find it in Toulouse, France in the Musee des Augustins.

Many of the paintings of Cleopatra focus on her death.

Cleopatra in the Movies

Over the years, there were a lot of different movies made about Cleopatra. The first one is called *Antony and Cleopatra.* This movie was done in 1908 and had Florence Lawrence in the leading roll. The plot focused on Antony and the Romans and Cleopatra had a supporting role. The next one, that focused more on Cleopatra as the main character, is called *Cleopatra, Queen of Egypt,* and was released in 1912.

Some of the other films that were released about Cleopatra over the years include:

- *Cleopatra* (1917)—This one was loosely based on several popular plays, including Shakespeare's version.
- *Cleopatra* (1934)—This version won an Academy Award.
    - *Caesar and Cleopatra* (1846)
    - *Serpent of the Nile* (1953)
- *Cleopatra* (1963)—This is probably one of the best loved versions of Cleopatra even today. It started Elizabeth Taylor, Richard, Burton, and Rex Harrison. It is another Academy Award winner.
- *Carry on Cleo* (1964)—This film was a spoof of the famous 1963 version.

- *Antony and Cleopatra* (1974)—This was one of the only versions that was performed through the Royal Shakespeare Company.
- *Cleopatra* (1999)— Unlike the other variations on Cleopatra's life, this one was based on historical facts. It is based off Margaret George's book.

There is just so much to know and love about Cleopatra. She was a brave queen who took on the world without batting an eye. She was a woman who knew that she could save her country and make it great again, something that was hard for a woman in a male dominated world. Her life was a romantic and adventurous story.

And the neat thing is, people are still talking about her. There are always new paintings, literature, and movies about this woman. The portrayals of Cleopatra help to show just how amazing she really was and the impact she has made on the whole world.

Chapter 11: The Legacy of Cleopatra

Cleopatra had a big impact on the society that she lived in. During this time, the men were the ones ruling the whole world. They had conquered lands, fought each other, and basically done everything in their own way. But Cleopatra was different. Even though she was a woman, she knew that she wanted to rule her own country and keep Egypt free and independent.

The idea of Cleopatra does not end with the romantic plays or history books that she is a part of. Her legacy still has a lot of value. Although Antony and Caesar were prominent figures, Cleopatra has always stood out on her own and not in connection with the other two.

Many people feel that Cleopatra really has nothing to do with our modern world. They feel that the media and all of the publications have turned Cleopatra into nothing but a story that people can fall in love with. While most know that Cleopatra was a historical figure, the queen of Egypt, and that she killed herself when she found out that her lover, Mark Antony, died, most know nothing else about this amazing queen.

Because the public knowledge about Cleopatra is limited and is based off what they have heard in books, movies, and plays, it is no wonder that most people have no idea about the legacy that Cleopatra left behind. They think that she was just a young girl in love. But there is so much more to Cleopatra and her life and that is why her legacy is still living on, even though more than 2000 years have passed.

So why was Cleopatra so important? This was not a time for Egypt. It was the time of the Roman Empire. The ancient Greeks had fallen and now the world was ruled by the Romans. Egypt was only unique in the fact that it provided more benefit to this empire as an independent nation than as one that was ruled by Rome. And Cleopatra was simply the ruler who was able to keep this all going. This might be important to her and her country, but on a worldwide scale, it did not mean much.

Still, Cleopatra was someone to reckon with on the world stage. The fact that she is the last ruler before the Romans took over earns her a big spot in the history books. She worked hard in order to keep Egyptian heritage strong. The Ptolemaic family had received Egypt after conquest, but for the most part they had allowed Egypt to stay the same. They didn't learn the customs or the language. Because of this, the people of Egypt saw very little change.

Cleopatra took this a step further than her ancestors. She decided that it was her job to protect the nation's heritage. She first did this by learning the language and the culture that were so important to her people, something that no one else in her family had taken the time to do. This allowed her to write legal documents in the Egyptian language, do paintings in this style, and help to keep that language around for many more years to come.

In addition, the fact that Cleopatra was able to keep Rome away is a huge testament to how much she valued the Egyptian people. With her close relationships and even marriage into Rome, it would have been really easy for Cleopatra to sell out her people to Rome for the promise of prestige and a nice title. She probably would have faired much better taking this deal. But Cleopatra was a strong woman and knew that her people were more important. No matter what offers she was able to get during her time in Rome, she always maintained that she was the queen of Egypt and worked her wiles in order to keep Egypt free until her death.

Why was Cleopatra so interested in keeping this heritage strong? For the most part, people believe that Cleopatra recognized that Egypt was one of the oldest sources of civilization. She liked the history of the area and the richness that came from the culture and wanted to preserve that from the new world that was forming thanks to the Romans. No matter what the reason was, though, she strived to keep Egypt free and independent for as long as she could.

Cleopatra was not a perfect person, especially when it came to morality and family, as was shown a lot with her story. First, let's look at morality. She was born in a time when it was the woman's job to bow down to the man. This did not happen. In fact, she was changed the roles that women held in her country by how she acted in regards to her brother. This was extremely against morals of the time.

Next, she became the mistress of Caesar while she was a married woman, even if her husband was her brother. In addition, she and Caesar ended up having a child together out of wedlock, when both were married to other people. While this didn't stop Caesar from trying to find a way to make his son the heir to Rome, it still was not considered the moral thing to do.

After Caesar died, she moved on to Antony. Antony was also a married man when he met Cleopatra. Rather than just stepping aside and letting him be with his wife, a choice that might have saved Egypt and kept Rome out of some wars, she and Antony decided to be together. This resulted in Antony leaving his wife, while she was pregnant, and having three children with Cleopatra.

Now let's take a look at how she treated her family. She was not the nicest person to her family. Rather than sharing the rule with her brother and husband, she treated him like he meant nothing. When he tried to exile her, Cleopatra used Caesar to get her place back. She was more than happy to fight against her younger brother and never showed any sorrow or mourning for his death.

When Caesar died, Cleopatra was quick to cause harm to the others in her family. She knew that her throne would be questioned and that she no longer had the protection of the great Caesar. This caused her to kill off her second brother as well as her sister in order to ensure that no one would try to take over the throne.

It can be argued that Cleopatra needed to do these things in order to maintain her throne and keep Egypt independent. While that might be true, they don't paint a picture of a very scrupulous woman.

But despite not having the most savory of pasts, Cleopatra was good for her country. She was able to keep it safe. Some of her other ancestors may have preferred to submit to the Romans. But Cleopatra was not able to do. While the men would be able to start wars and to fight, Cleopatra was a woman and had to find other means to persuade Rome to her side.

Cleopatra was able to do this by using her personal charms. She not only seduced Caesar and Mark Antony, but she had children with them and attempted to put her son on the Roman throne.

A man would not have been able to do this. A man would be expected to fight and hope that his army was stronger than the others. But Cleopatra came at the enemy from a different angle and this might have been what saved them.

In Cleopatra's story, there are no other major women figures. The only time they are discussed is if they are being killed. None of them were rulers and none of them were influencing leaders. While there were probably a few who were bending the ears of their spouse, most were supposed to sit back contently and do what the men wanted.

But this is not the way that Cleopatra wanted things to happen. She refused to be a backseat player. She didn't care that the world was dominated by men. In fact, she wasn't that good at communicating with other women and often made enemies of them. But when it came to men, Cleopatra could show them one big smile and they would all melt. Cleopatra knew that this could be her weapon.

Armed with her wit and charm, Cleopatra was ready to take on the world and make a big difference. If she had been able to stay on Octavian's good side and hadn't promoted her own children in a way that threatened the king, she might have lived longer.

One of the biggest legacies that Cleopatra left behind was that she was able to do so much for the Egyptian nation. Most argue that no man would have been as successful as this queen. She was able to keep Egypt free by showing how valuable they were to Rome. She was able to keep her throne all to herself despite the fact that others were all working against her. She showed women that they could be independent, and that while they might have to do things slightly differently than the men, they could be even more effective in their positions. Within her own country, she was able to lower taxes while still increasing the standard of living.

Another part of Cleopatra's legacy is the race rivalry. People were always wondering which side would win, the Romans or the Egyptians. But Cleopatra preferred cultural fusion rather than competition between the races. It is believed that Cleopatra thought everyone would do better working together rather than fighting.

Even though the thing Cleopatra is most remembered for is the romantic story of her death, she made a huge impact on the world. She was able to step up and show the world that a woman is able to rule and she is probably the only person during that time who could have made such an impact. She has a long-lasting legacy that is found even today and will probably be around for many years to come.

Chapter 12: The Fate of Egypt Following Cleopatra's Death

After Cleopatra died, things began to go into turmoil. First, Octavian was not happy when he found out that the young queen had died. He had hoped that he would be able to take both her and Antony back to Rome with him. Both Antony and Cleopatra were well-loved and famous, and many citizens of Rome, even those who claimed loyalty to Octavian, loved the young couple and wouldn't have minded having these two as rulers.

Octavian knew this and had planned to use their captivity as a symbol of his strength. It would scare his detractors by showing them that he would stop at nothing to catch and destroy them.

There was already a plan for a great celebration when Octavian came back to Rome. He had sent word that Antony and Cleopatra had fled from the war and that he was the victor. It was up to Octavian to finish up the fight, take over the capital of Egypt, and catch Antony and Cleopatra in order to bring them home. There was no way to save Egypt.

When Octavian found out that Cleopatra and Antony were dead, he was not happy. His next move was to deal with the children of Cleopatra. He started with Caesarion. Octavian thought of Caesarion as his biggest competition. Technically, Caesarion was not only the king of Egypt, he was also the only son of Julius Caesar. Octavian had often worried that Caesarion would decide that he wanted to take over Rome and he would come to claim the throne.

Actually, Caesarion never showed any interest in taking the throne. He was content working as a co-ruler of Egypt with his mother. It seems that this issue was mostly in Octavian's head. Cleopatra and Caesarion had given up on this plan years before, when Caesar died. Apart from Antony, no one wanted to lead a coup against the Roman throne on Caesarion's behalf.

Despite the evidence that Caesarion never wanted the throne, Octavian became worried that the plan would change, or at least that Caesarion would seek out revenge against the man that killed his mother. After he found out about Cleopatra's death, he had Casearion killed as well, thus ending the life of the last king of Egypt.

There is some debate as to whether Cleopatra was the last monarch in Egypt or her son but it is widely held that Cleopatra was the last pharoah. Shortly after her death, the kingdom of Egypt was taken over by Rome; Caesarion had no chance to effect change.

Once Casearion was dead, the rule of the Ptolemaic dynasty was ended. Octavian went back to Rome with Cleopatra's younger three children in tow and made them undergo the parade through the streets that he had planned for their parents. These children were still young and many felt sorry for their treatment.

Octavian made up for this later, somewhat. He allowed the chains to be taken off for the remainder of the parade. Once the celebrations were over, Octavian made sure that the three remaining children of Cleopatra and Antony were taken care of. His sister, the first wife of Antony, Octavia, took custody of the three children. It is said that she raised and educated them properly right along with her own children.

There is not much that is known about these three children after they made it to Rome. It is believed that the two boys died after living quiet lives. Cleopatra's daughter made a good marriage, and she was even allowed to rule with her husband in this new area. Despite how well they were treated, however, the children were never allowed to go back to Egypt, and it would be many years before that country became independent again.

As for Cleopatra and Antony, it is unsure where they are buried. While Cleopatra had her own tomb in Alexandria, it is commonly believed that she was buried right next to Antony, so that the two could travel to the spirit world together. No one has been able to recover the bodies. Whether this is because the two were buried in secret to keep them away from the desecration of Octavian, or whether the graves were just not disclosed, is uncertain. Some think that the two were buried near their home in Rome and others think they would have been left in Egypt and are probably near Alexandria.

The fate of Egypt was sealed shortly after Cleopatra died. Without a strong leader, it was easy to see that Rome was going to take over Egypt. The connections that Cleopatra had made were not set up to last after she was gone. It took no time at all for Egypt to fall to Rome and it stayed a Roman province until the Empire fell.

Chapter 13: The Earliest Known Days of Cleopatra

Cleopatra was the last ruler and queen of the dynasty of Macedonia. The line of rule she sprang from had been around since 323 B.C. when Alexander the Great passed, and would continue on unmatched in power until 30 B.C. when Rome prevailed. A woman of legend, her name will not soon be forgotten even though thousands of years have passed.

Cleopatra's Parents

This historical figure's family ruled over ancient Egypt for over a century before Cleopatra VII Thea Philopator was born in 69 B.C. The threat of the Romans would dominate her life exactly as it had dominated the life of her father. Cleopatra was no stranger to hardship, and instead of letting this intimidate her or make her weak she turned it to her distinct advantage and became a legend. She was the second born of five siblings, her father being Ptolemy XII Neos Dionysos who had been in power over Egypt since Ptolemy X Alexander II passed in 80 B.C.

Although no one knows for sure who Cleopatra's mother was, historians have surmised as to her identity and the likelihood that she was King Ptolemy XII's sister, Cleopatra V Tryphena. There have also been suggestions that Cleopatra's mother was King Ptolemy XII's half-sister or cousin, though we can never know for sure. The reason this is suspected is that there is lot of evidence that points to her mother being of Egyptian descent and quite possibly related to a high priest at the Ptah temple, the creator god who gave her father the crown and who was considered the most important of all priests during that time.

Ptolemy XII's Death and what it meant for Cleopatra

In 51 B.C. Cleopatra's father, Ptolemy XII, passed away and left the throne to his 18 year old daughter and her younger sibling, 10 year old Ptolemy XIII. Much is unknown about her early years, similar to the mystery of who her mother was. We do know that she seemed to appear suddenly on the scene of history some time near 50 B.C. and become a successful young queen, fully capable of rivaling her competitors.

She was more than able to keep up with the Romans and engage their interest - including the interest of Julius Caesar - but how she came to be such a capable leader is largely a mystery to us due to the blank spot in history concerning her formative childhood and teenage years. What can be known for sure is that she possessed a remarkable level of intelligence and cunning, or she never would have made it as far as she did.

There have also been extensive debates throughout history about the ethnicity of Cleopatra VII. While many believed for centuries that she was Greek, others suspect that she may have been of black African descent. Regardless of the race she was, her power was unmistakable and women and men of all races can be inspired by her. It has been said that the young queen married her brother, since that was not uncommon during those times. In the following years their home country of Egypt went through a number of struggles including economic issues, floods and widespread famine.

Cleopatra's Mysterious Upbringing 69 – B.C.

Legends state that Cleopatra was such a success because of her sexuality and physical appeal, but other sources point to her charm and intelligence as being responsible for her legacy. While many stories focus on her exceptional physical beauty, others claim that she was average looking. This remarkable woman was rumored to speak, or at least be able to understand, up to eight different languages. She was also reported to be the first royal in the entire dynasty to learn the language of Egyptian, which is what her subjects spoke. It is also supposed that she was an author who wrote extensively on subjects including cosmetics, measures and weights and possibly even magic.

From this, we can surmise that although we don't know the details of her upbringing, her formative years included a quality education. Not only does her knowledge of languages and writing skills point to this, but her successful strategizing later on in her ruling proves that she was no stranger to academics and critical thinking and must have had more great tutors than historians are even aware of from a young age.

In the second and third centuries of ancient Egypt, famous scholars and poets were often the tutors of princesses and princes in the Ptolemaic system. Historians assume that Cleopatra and her brother were no exception, since she educated her own kids in that fashion. Nikolaos of Damascus, the famous philosopher and historian, was the tutor she hired for the twin children she had with her husband, Mark Antony, in 40 B.C.

Though it can be assumed she had notable tutors that contributed to her education, the most influential teacher of her time was most likely Ptolemy XII- her own father. Intellectual training is all well and good for shaping a young mind, but where Cleopatra gained a true advantage was from being able to directly observe and learn from the experiences of her dad.

Chapter 14: Her Father and how his Ruling Affected Her

Cleopatra's father was obsessed with retaining his throne by any means necessary. Ptolemy XII had an intense interest in Dionysos, the Greek god of music and wine, whom the people of Greece related to Osiris who was the Egyptian royal deity. In addition to his interests in playing Dionysiac music on his flute he had passionate religious views, some of which drew criticism from historians in later years.

Ptolemy XII's Influence on her Later Strategies

Though his young daughter likely didn't understand very much of her father's religious views and the theology at the foundation of them, she was observant of the effects of this on his court. It possessed qualities of musical inspiration and sensuality and is thought to have contributed to her intelligent uses of spectacles of religion to advance her political career later on in life. To be a successful leader one must be able to relate to all types of people, and this was a skill Cleopatra learned early on and benefited from throughout her years of life.

The most important contributions Ptolemy XII made to his daughter's education, however, were through his own struggles concerning politics in a practical sense. She watched him learn harsh lessons about fighting to maintain his position of power in the face of constant competition both from his own family members and from ambitious politicians of Rome.

Ptolemy XII had a grip on his throne, but there were constant threats to this from the very moment he seized it in 80 B.C. The man was an illegitimate son to his father, Ptolemy IX, and he was constantly being challenged and having his ruling rights questioned. Among those who questioned him were politicians of Rome who saw Egypt as a valuable prize to be stolen and even made claims that the last legitimate king of Egypt, Ptolemy X Alexander II, had signed his empire to Rome in the case that he died without an heir.

The dangers the will of Ptolemy X posed become apparent in the year 63 B.C., when young Cleopatra was only seven. A man named P. Servilius Rullus, a tribune of Rome, suggested that the people of Rome annex the great nation of Egypt as was requested in Ptolemy X's will. He then suggested that they take over the rich farming land of Egypt to support a scheme that he claimed was intended to give land to the needy people of Rome.

Given this man's track record, it was hard to know whether he was being truthful about his pure intentions to help the poor of Rome and people were skeptical of what he truly intended to do with the land. This could have seriously altered the structure of the city and been dangerous.

Luckily for Ptolemy XII, however, the Roman tribune Rullus' attempts to pass this legislation were not successful. Politics in Rome in the mid and later parts of the 60s B.C. were largely controlled by the Romans' fearing Pompey. Pompey had recently defeated Mithridates VI of Pontus and was working on creating a prestigious reputation for himself, along with a loyal following, as he ran a successful campaign in the Near East region.

Rullus made claims about intending to help the Roman citizens, but his true motivation in the schemes he suggested were helping Pompey. He would have done this by giving him an efficient military command for the rivals of Pompey; Gaius Julius Caesar and Marcus Licinius Crassus. His attempts at gaining property were mostly for selfish reasons, or to support the questionable tyrant who would eventually be overthrown and taken over.

Ptolemy XII's Will and Determination to have his Children Inherit his Throne

The long and varied reign of Ptolemy XII ended similarly to how it started; fraught with fears and concerns about who would succeed the throne. He had his children deified and appointed Cleopatra to rule alongside him, which clearly highlighted the fact that he wished for his children to be his successors. However these actions did not help to get rid of the danger that Rome was posing against Egypt, which was gaining even more traction due to the large debts Ptolemy XII had accumulated during his attempts to maintain his throne.

Similarly to the ruler who preceded him, Ptolemy X, he crafted a will that favored the people of Rome- not naming them as heirs but as the mass guardians of his daughter Cleopatra and his oldest son Ptolemy XIII. The two siblings were to be married and take over his throne as siblings and partners, ruling Egypt together.

As soon as he deposited a single copy of the written will in the city of Alexandria for safety purposes and sent the second to Pompey, who was given the task of presenting it at the Senate, the ruler Ptolemy XII passed away in the year 51 B.C. during the springtime. He had done everything possible to ensure the survival of his ruling bloodline and dynasty, and once that had been completed it was time to go.

Chapter 15: How Cleopatra Seized the Throne

Ptolemy XII had the intention that his children would rule together, the way that Cleopatra and he had. However, this was not very likely to happen. Cleopatra, though still quite young at the time, was nearly 10 years older than her brother and her observations of her father and general life in the 50s B.C. had gotten her ready to face a powerful position.

Her younger brother Ptolemy XIII was still a child, and only had life experiences of events that had taken place in the Alexandria palace he lived in, whereas Cleopatra had already seen a lot and gained knowledge during her teen years from watching her father struggle politically and strategize about ruling. She saw him face challenges and overcome them, as well as determinedly maintaining his throne in the face of constant threat. An observant and intelligent girl, she had learned much from this and was fit to rule even at her young age.

Learning from her Father's Mistakes and Successes

Cleopatra had been present for the humiliating attempts the Romans had made to overthrow or manipulate her father and had observed his suffering. The young woman had also seen Ptolemy XII's brilliant return to the throne in the year 54 B.C., and the revenge he had enacted out of fear toward her sister and those who supported her. Perhaps it is not so surprising that young Cleopatra didn't take long to reveal that she had no intention of sharing her throne. Instead of giving in to her brother's supremacy as was the intention of her father, she would carry out different plans- rejecting the plans the court faction and Pothinos the eunuch had for her.

Not long after her father's passing, Cleopatra made sure to assert her claim to sole ownership of the throne. She adopted the name Thea Philopatora (which translates to "Goddess who loves her father"), which was cleverly selected to make it sound as though he had wished for her to be the real successor of his throne. In addition to this, Cleopatra had worked hard to garner support for her sole ownership of the throne in the upper area of the country where her dad had a strong support system. For nearly 200 years, Upper Egypt (Thebaid in particular) had been a large source of unrest in Egypt.

Starting around 80 B.C., Ptolemy X had taken great lengths to suppress a rebellion of the natives near there, ruining a large portion of Thebes with his brutal methods. Similar to many of the pharaohs that came before him, Ptolemy XII had sought out support in that area by supporting and aiding extravagant building of temples in the sanctuary areas. He knew that this would be a beneficial move, and his intuition was not mistaken.

He also made sure to cultivate the noble and priestly family sectors in the area, who considered government offices and temple structures as family heirlooms of great importance. He was careful in his strategizing and built support through careful means that took time and effort, and Cleopatra saw her opportunity to use his efforts to her advantage. There was never a moment that she was not looking for strategic moves to improve her chances at achieving goals, which is one of the factors that made her such a fantastic and effective leader.

Cleopatra's Early Strategizing and Garnering of Support of Upper Egypt

In 52 B.C., the elderly Buchis bull died and priests of Egypt discovered a new bull to take its place. The resourceful and new ruler saw a great chance with this event and seized this opportunity to continue her father's successful and popular policies in the upper region of Egypt. Both Romans and Greeks alike were typically fascinated by the Egyptian ways of religion, but their puzzlement and shock in response to cults of animals that were considered sacred was unmatched. Nearly every god was believed by Egyptian religion to have the potential to appear in specific animals.

Near the closing of the first millennium B.C., the Egyptians' reverence for holy animals had reached the point of centrality for popular cults in the area and people's devotion often took quite extreme modes of expression. Diodoros, the ancient historian who was reported to have visited Egypt in 60 B.C., watched a Roman embassy member get ripped apart by an angry group of mobbing people because he had killed a feline by accident.

A sacred and holy spot in the religion of Egyptians, however, was taken up by a select few animals who people claimed were the reincarnated versions of certain deities. These animals were recognizable by specific markings and, for this reason, stood out to people. When one of these animals died, a successor would be sought out and discovered and a period of great celebrations would follow the joyous event. These animals were treated as royal, pharaoh-like beings during their lives, and once they died they were given special burial treatment. These sacred animals were mummified and decadently buried in catacombs underground, as if they were kings.

How the Buchis Bull Helped Cleopatra Win Loyalty

The Buchis bull mentioned earlier was one such "reincarnated" animal, and exceptionally famous when compared to others. This bull could be recognized by his white body, black colored face and the direction his hair growth took (backwards). People everywhere claimed that this holy bull could change his colors as often as every hour, at will. The Egyptians believed that Buchis the bull was the reincarnated soul of the solar god Montu of Hermonthis, which was a city close to Thebes. Cleopatra, the young and ambitious new ruler, took the chance she saw with the installation of the second version of Buchis the bull in 51 B.C. This was her chance to take over and benefit from the loyalty of those who supported her father in Upper Egypt.

Her attempts were a great success, and years later as her conqueror (Augustus the emperor of Rome) reigned, everyone would recall how the goddess who loves her father, the Lady of the Two Lands, rowed Buchis the bull in an Amun barque, joining with the king's boats and all of the citizens of the city of Thebes.

The priests and Hermonthis were with him, which made the event all the more special to the inhabitants of the city with their great reverence for incarnated deities in animal form.

It is unclear whether Cleopatra herself held the same beliefs as these citizens, or whether this was only a clever tactic to gain support from Upper Egypt. Either way, it was a strategic and successful move that would benefit her later on and showed great promise of her capabilities as a ruler. It was smart moves like this that shaped her as a fearless and impacting leader who would be remembered for all time. There would be many more intelligent choices like this later on in her days of ruling.

Cleopatra's Interactions and Intentions with Thebaid

This remarkable woman was also able to secure support from the aristocracy of Upper Egypt, which included Kallimakhos the governor of the Thebaid. This was an impressive feat, as this man was considered essentially a viceroy who ruled the upper part of Egypt. Cleopatra was ambitious and determined in her ventures into Upper Egypt and because of this was wildly successful. She was so successful in this venture that the Thebaid offered to support her through the conquest of Egypt from Octavian in 30 B.C. and remained loyal to her throughout her entire, substantial reign.

Although this was a significant gain for Cleopatra and benefited her a lot, the main political power of Egypt in the Ptolemaic era did not lie in the Thebaid. It lay instead in Alexandria, the capital city, whose active and assertive body of citizens had seen the rise and fall of countless kings over the century. Cleopatra, unfortunately, only had a few loyal supports in Alexandria- much to her disappointment.

The Greeks of Alexandria had seen Ptolemy XII as their first selection for the ruling king in the year 80 B.C., but regardless of this support his relations with them had taken on a bitter edge throughout the course of his time of rule. For this reason, his daughter and successor was the new target for their hostility and frustrations. Perhaps even worse than this for the citizens, the specific ambitions that Cleopatra held were in direct contradiction to her dynasty's closely held traditional values. Queens of the Ptolemaic era, including Cleopatra I and Arsinoe II, had held a substantial amount of influence in this era but this was just as the regent or consort of the rule of a king. What this meant was that Ptolemy XIII, Cleopatra's brother, received the support of loyalists to the Ptolemaic rule, instead of the ambitious ruler herself.

Among these Ptolemaic loyalists were a sector known as the Gabinians, who were largely responsible for keeping Cleopatra's father on his throne in the later years of his rule. Once he had died though, Cleopatra further frustrated and alienated these people by choosing to hand over multiple Gainians to Syria's governor to take responsibility for the murder of two of an important Roman politician's sons.

The First Hints of Cleopatra's Historical Success and Fame

Historical accounts of this time period only give a glimpse into the outline of Cleopatra's early struggles to gain power, in a very general way. It appears that in the early days her audacity and speed contributed largely to the success she would enjoy in the later years of her life. For the end of 51 B.C. and first portion of the year 50 B.C., her rise to power is made clear by the fact that Ptolemy XIII's name virtually started disappearing from all documents from that time period. Official papers stated nothing of him, which suggests that her power was unmatchable to her younger sibling and that she soon became the focus of the ruling throne.

As the era of 50 B.C. fell however, the new ruler's ambitious attempts at securing lone power of the throne were not very successful. Disastrous famines struck the nation of Egypt and caused a tragically low level of the Nile. This gave those who wished to defeat her the perfect chance to make their attempt. Enemies took this chance enthusiastically and were able to undermine her successful support in the upper part of Egypt, as well as get stronger and more loyal support from citizens of the capital city Alexandria.

There was an official decree passed in the fall of the year 50 B.C. under the names Cleopatra and Ptolemy XIII that gave orders to merchants to hand over grains gathered in Upper Egypt to the capital city, and even stated that violators of this new law would be sentenced to death.

Cleopatra was understandably desperate at this point, and it's been surmised that she attempted to secure a more easily compliant spouse in her brother Ptolemy XIV, who was essentially meant to replace Ptolemy XIII. This plan appears to have been foiled when she was made to escape from the capital city of Alexandra during the year 49 B.C. Cleopatra first took refuge near the Thebaid and eventually traveled to both southern Syria and Palestine, seeking out support from friends of her passed father.

The Faceoff at the Border and what it meant for Cleopatra

From here she went on to collect a decent, if small, army and returned to try to invade her home nation of Egypt. This ambitious advance only lasted a short while and she was caught at the border by forces of her royal sibling, Ptolemy XIII. These forces were in possession of one important fortress, the key of Pelusium, which allowed them to close off the road along the coast into Egypt from Sinai.

At this point she was probably getting even more desperate, and knew that her final demise was not only possible but likely. Perhaps it is quite ironic that she was then rescued by the unforeseen reappearance of Roman influence in the affairs of her home country Egypt.

It was true that the great nation of Egypt survived, but the amazing kingdom that had been inherited by Cleopatra was not as strong as it once was. It had been robbed of its possessions, gone through intense economic hardship and been inflicted with nearly constant strife in a dynastic sense. Regardless of those factors Egypt remained attractive to politicians of Rome, who saw it as a prize to be won. Starting from the day Cleopatra received the throne in 50 B.C., she fought to reverse the decline of the nation and had some major successes.

But even though the country's chances of improving appeared bleak and brightened as she reigned, the ruler was smart enough to see that staying independent from Rome was just not realistic or beneficial. She made sure Egypt was secure by making it absolutely necessary for Roman plans to be successful in the east of the Mediterranean. This was a large motivating force behind much of her efforts and strategies during her reign.

Chapter 16: Cleopatra and Julius Caesar

Plutarch records state that before Caesar had ever set foot in Theodotus at Egypt, Ptolemy XIII's tutor had ventured out to sea to meet him bringing along Pompey's severed head. This gesture was meant to gain favor with Julius Caesar and encourage him to head to Rome right away, since his business in Egypt could effectively be finished. The gesture, however, had quite the opposite effect that the tutor had hoped for. Julius Caesar was extremely angry about the murder of Pompey (who was his son in law), and saw it as cowardly and unnecessary.

There is a possibility that the intention of Caesar was to show Pompey mercy (which was customary in his interactions with enemies), since he openly wept when he saw the head and then immediately took steps to preserve it until it could be buried properly.

Another source hints at the possibility that Julius was planning to murder Pompey but was disappointed in the fashion in which it occurred- under a foreigner's orders- and perhaps his open weeping was exaggerated for politically beneficial reasons. Regardless of his exact reaction, it is sure that this event contributed to his ill feelings for Ptolemy XIII.

Not long after this, Pothinus, who guarded Ptolemy XIII and is said to have been the strongest force behind the throne, successfully enraged a mob in Alexandria against Julius Caesar but Caesar did not get intimidated easily. Instead Julius landed with a force that was small but powerful and headed up to the palace. Caesar then commanded that Cleopatra and Ptolemy were to release their armies and took it upon himself to remind Pothinus that Ptolemy Auletes' heirs had a debt of 6000 talents to him (a substantial amount of money.)

The Legendary Meeting of Cleopatra and Caesar

Pothinus did not appreciate this defiance to his orders (since he was the chancellor of Egypt, he controlled the nation's finances at the time) and did not bother to hide his insolent feelings towards Caesar, which ended up having devastating consequences for the man he was supposed to have been guarding- Ptolemy. Cleopatra, again always seeking opportunity and advantage, saw a chance to benefit. She was determined to seize the opportunity of Pothinus' mistake and even arranged a meeting in secret with Julius Caesar. Plutarch reveals a legendary story that states that the brave woman hid in a carpet roll until she could reveal herself to Caesar, and then presented herself in a veil.

It may have been her beauty, or her prestigious lineage (she was descended from Alexander the Great). It may have been her charisma or courage that charmed Julius, but from this point on the two became lovers. Julius reversed his decision right away about

Pompey, and instead gave power back to Cleoopatra and her brother. Whatever it was that she did to win him over and gain his trust and admiration, it undoubtedly worked well.

When her brother showed up to meet with Caesar, he saw his sister in a relaxed state in the chambers and ran off completely enraged. This could have been jealousy either over his sister's affections or her own brilliant strategizing. Either way, Ptolemy XIII stormed out of the palace in a fit of rage, yelling about being betrayed by his sister and attempting to stir up a mob to defeat Cleopatra and Julius Caesar.

Despite these attempts, Caesar was a great speaker and was able to calm the crowd down by presenting Ptolemy Auletes' will, which stated that the brother and sister should have the throne together. He also officially named their even younger siblings (Arsinoe and Ptolemy XIV) as the rulers of an area Rome had recaptured not long before that, Rhodes. The decision to give Rhodes back to Egypt was not taken well by the citizens of Rome, but it was a strategic move by Julius set forth with the intentions of buying more time, securing his new lover's gratitude and undermining Ptolemy XIII and Pothinus' possible attempts to rebel against him by stirring up mobs.

The Banquet of Julius Caesar and the Dangerous Turn it took

Julius Caesar decided to hold a banquet to celebrate the decision of appointing the siblings as joint rulers. He had the displeasure, however, of discovering that Pothinus and Achillas were planning to defeat him. In response to this discovery, Caesar commanded that the banquet hall be surrounded by his army men and had Pothinus executed right then and there. Achillas, Ptolemy's general who had been helping him plan to defeat Caesar, was able to escape and rally Ptolemy's troops (only freshly back from Pelusium) and the Greeks of Alexandria who made up the guard of the town. The army had the palace surrounded but Julius, aware of the fact that he was in a tough spot, stayed indoors with his lover Cleopatra holding a hostage; Ptolemy XIII.

Caesar was aware of the fact that he was seriously outnumbered but he knew that he had aid on its way to help him- reinforcements from the Levant and Anatolia. In addition to this he was aware that Achillas would attempt to prevent them from helping, so as he organized a last minute defense of his palace he gave an order that every ship in the harbor be set on fire.

The flames reached warehouses on the nearby shorelines and Arsinoe, Cleopatra's sister, was able to escape with Ganymedes her tutor. Arsinoe then joined up with Achillas who succeeded to name her Egypt's Queen. She quickly responded to this by having him murdered when he disagreed with a decision she made, and replacing him with Ganymedes.

As the chaos continued outside the palace, Ganymedes plotted to poison the supply of water to Caesar's palace and arranged a way to cut the palace off using road blocks. However Cleopatra was aware of all of the local water course locations and the newer wells were cut off quickly. Caesar chose a tactical move of allowing Ptolemy to go free, hoping that Arsinoe and Ptolemy would fight and both become weakened. Unfortunately for Julius the siblings were able to look past their rivalry with the goal of defeating Caesar and Cleopatra in mind, which only strengthened the army of Ptolmy and the guard of Alexandria.

At this point we can assume that Cleopatra was getting a bit concerned about her luck running out, but it appears that Julius never even considered giving her over to the enemies for his own benefit. The reasons for this are uncertain; it could have been due to his own bravery but many believe that it was mostly because he had recently found out that Cleopatra was pregnant and expecting a son.

The Dramatic Closing of the Battle at the Palace

Things were looking dire for the couple, but just when everything appeared to be looking too bad the reinforcements of Caesar showed up and engaged in an intense battle. After this they took over the causeway which lined the Great Lighthouse to Caesar's palace. Just then another wave of reinforcements appeared, the army of the Prince of Pergamon, and Caesar had further support. This meant that Ptolemy had no choice but to go south and face the army.

Julius led his army out to pursue, teaming up with his allies of Pergamon and engaging in a battle which led to Ptolemy being drowned and defeated in the Nile River. Upon his death, Julius retrieved Ptolemy's body from the Nile and began heading to the capital city of Alexandria to make Cleopatra aware of his success. She showed up to meet him, leading an impressive procession of gods and sacred symbols. Rumors say that she was dressed up to emulate Isis, her favorite goddess, and was no doubt stunning to behold.

Upon meeting his lover, Julius Caesar officially named her younger sibling Ptolemy XIV as the ruler alongside her. This would ensure that her right to the throne was secure. After this he married her in the typical Egyptian way, but their union was not considered official in Rome since he had already been married to someone else and it was considered illegal for citizens of Rome to marry someone from another country.

The Celebration Following the Marriage of Julius and Cleopatra

The newlyweds took a cruise down the Nile River to celebrate their honeymoon. This gave Cleopatra an opportunity to show the Egyptian people that she was completely in charge and also for her to show her new husband her homeland. This honeymoon cruise was probably also meant to be a journey toward the land of Edfu, where she could establish a connection between her young son Caesarion and the god Horus, which would ensure his fate as the leader of Egypt in the future.

As the couple began their return to the capital city of Alexandria, Julius started to plan his return to his homeland of Rome. The citizens of his homeland criticized him quite harshly for his failure to take over Egypt and add it to the empire. They also criticized Caesar for staying in Egypt for too long after Ptolemy XIII's death in the river. In Rome there were quite a few factions who had maintained their loyalty to the fallen Pompey, some of whom involved his own sons. This meant that the ruler had a lot of matters of importance he needed to handle, including the necessity of visiting his Jewish allies and showing them appreciation for the support they provided during the war of Alexandria.

The ruler abandoned not one but three different legions in the capital city so he could support his wife, Cleopatra, while she established the status of Egypt and also to take Arsinoe as a prisoner back to Rome with him for her treasonous ways. In addition to this he handed over Cyprus to Cleopatra, which gave her the revenue necessary to lower taxes in Egypt while improving the economy at the same time.

The Birth of Their Son, Caesarion

Cleopatra had her son, Ptolemy XV Caesarion, in the summer of 47 B.C. In honor of this there was a decree set up in a specific version of hieroglyphs in Saqqara. In addition to this, the baby's lineage was announced and written on buildings and monuments across the nation (the Temple of Dendera was among these, depicting a famous scene). Julius appears to have been overjoyed at the birth of his son. Some people who worked under Caesar started looking into the idea of adjusting Roman law to assign his new son as the rightful heir, searching for ways around the laws against marrying people from different countries and his previous marriage.

Julius had a coin made that depicted the goddesses Aphrodite and Venus, and his wife Cleopatra also had a coin made that showed herself as Aphrodite and Venus nursing her new baby, Caesarion. In the year 46 B.C. she went to Rome, accompanied by her husband and brother, Ptolemy XIV, and her son (who Julius was still having a hard time getting recognized as his rightful heir to the throne).

They were all welcomed officially as allies and friends of the people of Rome, and assigned a villa at the Hill of Janiculum to live in which belonged to Caesar. The villa was very large and had a nice view of the nearby city and a fabulous garden area. Caesar did not live here with them however, and stayed with his original Roman wife, Calpurnia.

Since the Egyptian marriage between Julius and Cleopatra was not officially recognized by the law of Rome, Cleopatra became known as his mistress instead of his wife. She held multiple "symposia", where many people were invited to come and enjoy feasts and live poetry which was said to have made her popular with the friends of her husband. Cleopatra also seems to have had something to do with Mark Antony returning to the good graces of Caesar. He had been the deputy of Julius, but Lepidus was assigned to replace him due to his questionable and immoral habits. This could have been aided by the fact that Mark Antony enjoyed Greek culture and style and was rumored to be close with the Ptolemys.

Caesar's Choices for Statues and their Significant Placement

Julius had made a promise that stated that if he were to prevail against his enemy Pompey, he would erect a brand new temple to honor his divine ancestor, Venus Genetrix. Caesar put a statue made of bronze which depicted Alexander the Great's horse, Bucephalus, out in front of this structure and also had a gold statue of his lover, Cleopatra, placed next to the Venus statue in the middle of this temple.

It was not unusual for pharaohs of the Ptolemaic era to have statues depicting themselves placed right next to deities, but the practices of Rome were quite different and did not approve of placing a human's form alongside gods. This seemed to claim that she possessed special authority of a divine nature, which they did not approve of.

Also the goddess Venus was typically used to represent marriage, and the Roman citizens saw his choice of the Venus statue as an indirect but obvious statement about his marriage to Cleopatra. Julius also made sure to put statues depicting himself throughout Rome, including at the Romulus (the man who discovered Rome and was thus deified) temple.

Another state was titled "unvanquished god", a term people typically reserved for the revered Alexander the Great. Caesar was in charge of a large amount of construction activity, which usually involved the classic

Egyptian-Greek hybrid style and set his mind to erecting a giant Roman library to rival the biggest library that existed at the time (the Alexandrian Great Library).

Cleopatra's Irreplaceable Impacts on Roman Culture

The astronomers employed by Cleopatra aided Julius in creating the Julian calendar, which had never existed previously and was intended to take the place of the Roman calendar (which was rumored to be defective). The Julian calendar was to have a leap year and 365 days and is what we base our current, modern calendar on 0(with only small changes made by Pope Gregory, many years later). It is unquestionable that Cleopatra had a huge and unrivaled effect on the culture and art of Rome.

Regardless of these positive contributions to the culture of Rome, the relationship of Caesar and Cleopatra was not very popular with the senate of Rome. Calpurnia came from a strong and popular family in Rome and was demure and subservient, as was typical of Roman women at the time. Cleopatra on the other hand was the opposite; outspoken, ambitious and powerful. Julius had countless enemies during this time period, Cicero the orator being the main one and possibly the most menacing threat to him.

Cicero the orator officially named Alexandria as the home to all deceit and tricks, and made no secret of the fact that he hated Cleopatra. Cicero believed that females were inherently weak on an intellectual level and should look to and be under the guidance of their superior male guardians. For this reason, he was very unsettled about Caesar being so heavily influenced by Cleopatra.

Around this time, rumors began circulating that Julius had plans to switch the capital over to Alexandria; in essence adding to the power of Egypt at the expense of Rome. In response to these rumors, senators started coming up with plans for reversing the reforms of Caesar.

Julius Caesar and his Contributions to the City

It was the year 45 B.C. when Julius came upon Pompey's sons and had an intense and bloody battle with them that ended in his favor. Regardless of this success, the youngest son of Pompey was able to escape and Julius experienced a number of seizures in quick succession. These seizures concerned him quite a bit and motivated him to retire to Lavicum to live in his villa and start rewriting his will. He made sure to leave a few golden coins to each citizen of Rome and established the luxurious villa gardens at the hill of Janiculum as public park property.

He also left some of his wealth to Mark Antony and his nephew, Octavian. Though he had tried many times, he had still been unable to change Roman law to include his son Caesarion or wife Cleopatra in the will, but made sure to start a clause which assigned guardians to children who would be born in the future. This is thought to have been included because Cleopatra was pregnant again at this time.

As he headed toward Rome, he decided to stop and spend a couple of days with the orator, Cicero, in order to acquire information about the senate's opinion of his new changes. The senate had decided to name him as a lifelong dictator, but he wanted to go even further than this.

Conclusion

The story of Cleopatra has stunned people for many years. During a time and in a world that was dominated by men, in a time when the world was about to become one big empire, Cleopatra was a strong woman who was able to keep her kingdom independent. She knew what it took to be a strong leader and refused to back down. While she may not have been able to fight in the military like her male counterparts, she was able to make a stand and form ties and relationships in ways that weren't possible to other leaders.

There is something for everyone when it comes to the story of Cleopatra. Although she was just a young woman of 39 when she passed, she gave rise to enough stories and relationships to fill up many books. She married three times, kept her country independent and thriving after many years of hardship, and had relationships with two of the most important figures in the history of the Roman Empire. While there are a lot of great historical figures, no one can come close to all of the prestige and amazing stories about Cleopatra.

Many books have been written about this amazing character and the life that she lived. She was expected to just sit back and let others take the wheel. But the pages of history would not be the same if Cleopatra had been satisfied to sit back and just enjoy her privilege instead of actually ruling her country.

There is so much to learn and understand about the amazing Cleopatra. This guidebook has all the stories and information that you need to order to see how wonderful this woman was and why she is still such an iconic figure in todays world. Take a look through this book and see what else you can learn about the wonderful queen Cleopatra.

www.ingramcontent.com/pod-product-compliance
Lightning Source LLC
Chambersburg PA
CBHW050401120526
44590CB00015B/1783